PUB WA
— IN —
Norfolk

THIRTY CIRCULAR WALKS
AROUND NORFOLK INNS

Liz Moynihan

COUNTRYSIDE BOOKS
NEWBURY, BERKSHIRE

First published 1993
© Liz Moynihan 1993
Reprinted 1995, 1997, 1999

Revised and updated 2003

COUNTRYSIDE BOOKS
3 Catherine Road
Newbury, Berkshire

ISBN 1 85306 236 7

To view our complete range of books,
please visit us at
www.countrysidebooks.co.uk

Designed by Mon Mohan
Cover illustration by Colin Doggett
Photographs by the author
Sketch maps by Sarah Talks

Produced through MRM Associates Ltd., Reading
Typeset by Paragon Typesetters, Queensferry, Clwyd
Printed in England by J. W. Arrowsmith Ltd., Bristol

To Isobel

Contents

Publisher's Note

We hope that you obtain considerable enjoyment from this book; great care has been taken in its preparation. However, changes of landlord and actual closures are sadly not uncommon. We are anxious that all details concerning both pubs and walks are kept as up to date as possible, and would therefore welcome information from readers which would be relevant to future editions.

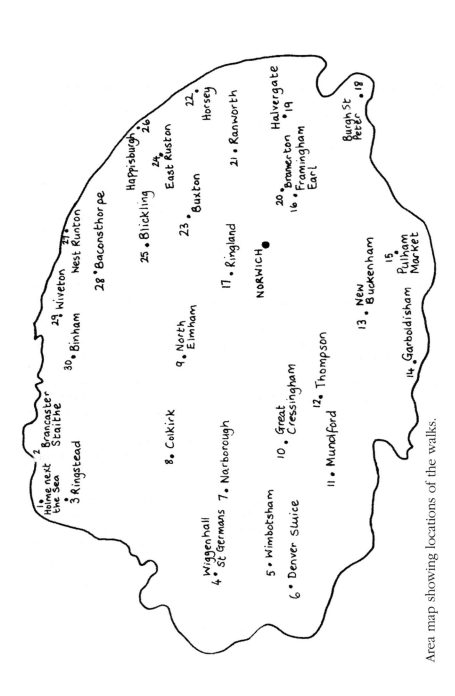

Area map showing locations of the walks.

Introduction

What could be nicer than an outing for all the family – a gentle walk through beautiful countryside with the prospect of a drink or pub meal in pleasant surroundings at the end. A good day out which will not cost the earth! Norfolk offers a wide variety of landscapes and is full of historical and topographical interest. This book attempts to sample a little of all that Norfolk has to offer by describing walks which give a flavour of the whole county, ranging from short village orientated strolls to longer rambles through wilder countryside. Distances mostly vary from 2 to 5 miles – easily coped with by the average child. There are some longer walks for the more energetic and opportunities for short cuts whenever possible. Some of these are obvious from the Ordnance Survey map; others are described in the text.

Most people think of Norfolk as totally flat. Certainly it has no mountains, but the landscape is a subtle blend of rolling countryside and wide open spaces. It ranges from wooded Breckland in the south to watery fenland in the north while the coast includes cliffs and stony beaches as well as large areas of saltmarsh and sand dune. Norfolk has an attractive, old fashioned and unchanging atmosphere, largely due to the fact that it is a county of large estates whose owners care for the hedges and woodlands and the heritage of their estate villages and cottages. Because of the wide range of habitats found in the county, the wildlife is diverse. Wild flowers abound and encourage some very special insects and butterflies. Take binoculars with you not only for the birdlife but also to make the most of the very wide views offered on some of the walks. One of the small joys of Norfolk is that each village has its own special sign which is carved or painted with scenes which indicate something of the community's history.

Although a very rural county, Norfolk has half as many footpaths as the national average, but it does have an inordinate number of lanes and byroads going nowhere in particular. There are also several long distance routes such as the Peddar's Way and the Norfolk Coast Path. In contrast many footpaths and bridleways on the Definitive Footpath Map have disappeared or are obstructed perhaps because the farming influence is paramount and the population is relatively sparse. Thus, in several of the walks in this book, lanes have been used as an alternative to impassable paths but they are generally very peaceful and little used by motor traffic. Wherever you walk please respect the countryside and follow the Country Code.

This book is all about exploring Norfolk. The pubs, which vary greatly in type and location, have been chosen as a centre for each walk and all provide a welcome drink and generally a sustaining meal. Many excellent pubs have had to be left out either because there is not a good walk near them or because they are too close to an area already covered in the book. All the publicans are very happy for you to leave your car in the car park while walking, provided you use the pub facilities at some stage – but do ask first. Alternative car parking is indicated whenever possible. As for opening times, the pubs seem to keep more or less to the traditional opening hours. Give or take ½ hour at each end, these are 11.30 am to 2.30 pm and 6 pm to 11 pm, Monday to Friday (12 noon to 3 pm and 7 pm to 10.30 pm on Sunday). Food is usually available between 12 noon and 2 pm and from 7 pm. It may be worth a phone call to check the times if you are travelling some distance.

Although sketch maps of the walks are given, you may well want to ramble further afield and it is helpful to have the relevant Ordnance Survey Landranger map to hand. Sheet numbers and grid references are given at the start of each walk. I have indicated other walks and places of interest in the vicinity of the walks described. Distances given are only an indication and not precise as I always have trouble with pedometers. So step out and enjoy yourselves – Norfolk has so much to offer!

Liz Moynihan

① Holme next the Sea
The White Horse

This traditional village pub once was an old farmhouse built in the late 17th century. It is close to the Peddar's Way which ends rather surprisingly in the small village of Holme and is also handy for walkers from the Norfolk Coast Path less than a mile away. There is a private caravan park behind the pub and a large walled lawn with a backdrop of trees to the side for al fresco eating and drinking.

The White Horse belongs to Pubmaster and has Flowers Original, Marston's Pedigree and other changing guest real ales. Dry Blackthorn cider is on draught. Well behaved dogs are allowed in the bar. There is no separate family room, but children accompanied by an adult are welcome. A blackboard on the wall advertises the day's specials and there is also a general menu. The main bar with its tiled floor is furnished traditionally and is awash with old beams, horse brasses and hunting horns. Round the corner is a cosy snug with a carpet and banquette seating.

The pub has a reputation for excellent bar meals. Everything is freshly cooked, of excellent quality, and there is plenty of it. The fish and chips are crisp and delicious and of such a size that the fish hangs off both ends of an oval platter. Freshness is guaranteed by using local sources so that the fish is virtually straight from the sea. Food is served at lunchtimes and evenings every day and all day during the summer season.

Telephone: (Holme) 01485 525512.

How to get there: The village of Holme next the Sea lies about 1 mile east of Hunstanton on the A149. The pub is in the centre of the village down a lane leading off the main road.

Parking: There is a car park to the side of the pub but this can be crammed in summer. Alternatively, cars can be parked in a field near the beach (payment required during the summer season).

Length of the walk: 4½ miles of fairly easy walking with some gentle uphill work. There is an opportunity for a short cut. OS Map Landranger series 132 North West Norfolk (GR 704435).

This delightful walk explores the pretty village of Holme, with its variety of old flint, cobble, clunch and carstone cottages huddled under pantiled roofs, and the green lanes with extensive sea and marsh views on the hillside behind the village. The walk joins the last mile or two of Peddar's Way on its journey to the sea and then travels along the Norfolk Coast Path for a short distance as it borders Holme beach. The walk can be extended here by continuing on through Holme Dunes Nature Reserve – a lovely area of varied habitat ranging from sandy beach, dunes, and pine shelter belt to saltmarsh and grazing marsh, all of which attracts a wide variety of flora and fauna. The diversity of birds is especially good. A short walk through the meadows of another bird reserve brings the walker back to base.

The Walk

Turn left out of the pub and walk along Kirkgate past the village hall and the church of St Mary on the left, distinguished by its tall tower and Nelson graves (relations of Lord Nelson who was born at Burnham Thorpe not far away). Follow the lane as it bends sharply to the right to become Eastgate, and carry on to the main A149 coast road.

Cross carefully and continue on up the broad stony track on the other side of the road passing the manor house on the right and then cottages on the left. Continue along this track (an old county road) as

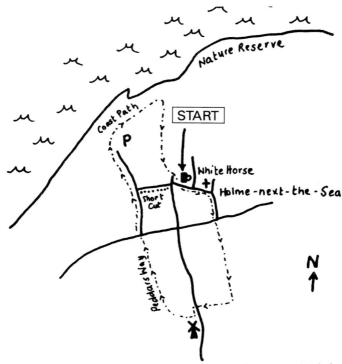

it ascends gently for about a mile sometimes between high banks and passing a wooded old pit on the right. Ignore all side tracks. This track eventually meets a cross track (Greenbank – another old county road) at the top of the slope (arrow marker on post).

Turn right along this and enjoy the extensive views over to Ringstead mill on the left, to the billowing woods of Old Hunstanton Hall ahead and later on down over fields to the marshes and the sea. When Greenbank meets a small metalled road, turn left for a short distance passing the sign for Ringstead, then turn right into a field alongside a hedgerow on the left following the signs for Peddar's Way.

Follow the narrow but well-trodden path round to the right at another marker post and continue on through fields, then alongside a hedge on the left. Eventually the path becomes a broad green lane, hedged on both sides, and descends gently to the main road again, passing to the left of a track to a bungalow. Cross carefully and continue on down the lane ahead (Peddar's Way signpost on the verge on the right). This thickly hedged lane bends gently. Ignore the turn to the right to Holme village (this could be used as a short cut leading back to the pub) and continue straight on down a winding lane crossing the river Hun near a caravan site and continuing on. Ignore

11

the stony road to the right which leads to the Holme Dunes Reserve and carry on past toilets on the left and a car park on the right. Cross the first part of the golf course then go through a gap by a gate crossing the next section on a board walk (look out for flying balls).

Before reaching the beach, follow the direction of the wooden footpath signpost which points out the Coast Path to the right. Pass a Holme Dunes Nature Reserve information board and follow a wide sandy track past a white-topped post. At another similar post look for the arrow marker on the right which points the path up onto a bank. Continue ahead with views over the marsh and dunes to the sea on the left and over brambles and scrub towards scattered houses on the right. The path goes onto a board walk. Just past a large house surrounded by stunted pines, the last building along the dunes, turn right down a cross-piece of board walk and go down a sandy slope bearing right to a stony track and the entrance gate of the Holme Dunes Reserve by a small wooden hut.

Go through the gateway onto the stony track and then go almost immediately left across a wooden bridge over the river Hun onto Redwell marsh (a Norfolk Ornithologists' Association Reserve). Continue ahead skirting the left hand edge of a meadow alongside a rough fence back in the direction of the village. Pass an unfenced area then pick up the fence by bushes again eventually bearing left to a metal gate and stile. Cross the stile and follow the track round to the right past cottages to the main street of Holme (Kirkgate) at a junction of lanes. Turn left back to the pub passing the village shop and post office on the right.

Brancaster Staithe
The Jolly Sailors

Walkers and birdwatchers are especially welcome here (there is a bird pager on the bar), but as befits its name, the Jolly Sailors in summer is stuffed full of intrepid dinghy sailors who pit their wits against the tidal creeks between Brancaster Staithe and Scolt Head Island. They suit the informal atmosphere of the main bar with its old tiled floors, its motley collection of wooden tables and settles, and its rough white-painted walls. This comfortable area is warmed in winter by an open fire. In addition, there is the small Harbour Bar, a family room full of traditional pub games and a creeper-wreathed covered loggia leading into the attractive garden at the side, where food and drink can be taken when weather permits. This award-winning pub is on the main A149 coast road not far from the staithe itself and you can't miss its homely white painted exterior.

A wide variety of excellent homemade bar food, including mussels in white wine and cream (the mussels come from the staithe only 100 yards away). Dishes of the day, which include seasonal fish, shellfish (including local oysters) and game, are put up on a blackboard. There is a separate home-made puddings menu. Food is served every day from 12 noon to 9 pm. Adjoining the restaurant is a more informal dining room, with tables covered in cheerful cloths, where families can eat and children can run in and out of the french door opening into the garden where there is a play area for their amusement whilst the grown ups relax after their meal.

The pub, a freehouse, serves Woodforde's Wherry, Adnams Bitter plus guest ales, with draught Guinness and Scrumpy Jack cider. It is open all day every day from 11 am, except for Christmas Day when it is open for drinks only from 12 noon to 3 pm. Dogs are welcome but not in the restaurant. The latter is a no smoking area.

Telephone: (Brancaster) 01485 210314.

How to get there: The Jolly Sailors is on the A149 coast road at Brancaster Staithe, midway between Hunstanton and Wells-next-the-Sea in north-west Norfolk.

Parking: The pub has its own large car park at the side and back or there is parking on the nearby staithe (watch out for the occasional exceptional high tide) or on Barrow Common.

Length of the walk: 3½ miles. OS Map Landranger series 132 North West Norfolk (GR 793444).

This lovely coastal walk through undulating gorse-scented common land and saltmarshes purple with sea lavender in summer offers spectacular views over thousands of acres of National Trust dunes and marshes and the Scolt Head Island Nature Reserve. This belongs to the Norfolk Wildlife Trust and the National Trust and can be visited by boat. Its special interest lies in the large colony of common and Sandwich terns which nest on the western tip. Between the marsh and the higher common land lies the site of Branodunum, the most northerly of the Saxon Shore forts built by the Romans as a defence against Anglo-Saxon raiders.

The Walk

Turn left out of the front door of the pub and walk to the left up a lane, passing scattered houses, coming eventually to Barrow Common, an unspoilt area of gorse, bracken and blackberries on the brow of the hill stretching to either side of the lane. (Take care when

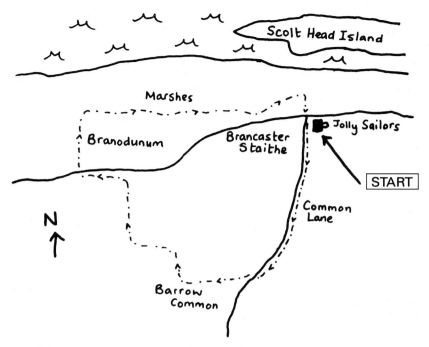

walking as the common is riddled with rabbit holes.) Pass a seat on the left (fantastic view from here) and continue on a little way to where a rough path goes to the right through the common, signposted to Branodunum. Walk ahead, avoiding all cross tracks and keeping roughly parallel to a line of trees on the right. Alternatively, pass a derelict hut on the right and walk along a path through the trees with views over the coast. At a main cross path bordered by a hedge turn right passing through a gateway and going downhill along a broad grassy track offering lovely views over the marshes. After veering left then right the hedged track continues downhill to meet the busy A149 coast road.

Turn left along a narrow pavement, then after a short distance cross the road and turn right down a narrow lane with high hedges on either side. Where the lane bends to the left, go straight on over a stile by a gate into the field of Branodunum, the site of an extensive Roman fort where the Dalmatian cavalry were once stationed to protect against raiders. The area belongs to the National Trust who have established permissive footpaths and erected an information board. Continue straight ahead across this field to another stile on the far boundary. Cross this onto the marsh. The muddy creeks and rich

15

plant life of the saltmarsh attract many ducks, geese and wading birds.

Turn right and walk along the edge of the marsh which extends towards Scolt Head Island way over on the left (be prepared for the path here to be uneven and soggy). The island is nearly 4 miles long and is continually changing shape according to wind and tide. There is a nature trail but visitors and dogs are not allowed near the ternery during the breeding season. Boats can be hired from the staithe to visit the island but the timing depends on the tide. Birds to look out for in this area include oyster catchers, ringed plover, redshank, greenshank, gannet, kittiwake and Arctic skua as well as the terns: Sandwich, Arctic, common and little, and a variety of geese and ducks. Continue on along the boarded marsh path (part of the Coast Path) past the odd converted barn to reach a fence and stile on the outskirts of Brancaster Staithe. Cross the stile and continue ahead past the back of a converted maltings (supposedly built partly from stone from the Roman fort) and the gardens of cottages to approach the green in front of The National Trust's Dutch gabled Dial House (a residential Activity Centre).

Instead of crossing the green, turn left by the edge of a creek skirting round the back of Dial House and bear right along a narrow fenced path which emerges onto Brancaster Staithe hard and harbour by the Trust's information and cycle hire centre. This is open at weekends from March to July, then daily in the July/August holiday season. In Victorian times the harbour could accommodate ships of 500 tons and operated as a busy port, but commercial activity, except for a few fishing boats, ceased as the harbour silted up, giving way to a mass of pleasure craft of all types. Cross the hard and continue straight on, passing the sailing club on the right and a creek on the left to reach a stony track by mussel fishermen's sheds. The Brancaster creeks provide a 'fattening ground' for tiny mussels brought from their breeding grounds in the Wash. The local fishermen have invested huge sums of money in a purification plant to comply with EEC regulations although the local harbour has been deemed pollution free. Turn right up the track which emerges onto the main road opposite the Jolly Sailors.

③ Ringstead
The Gin Trap

This popular 17th century coaching inn, set back from the road behind a huge chestnut tree, in the interesting village of Ringstead, is famous for its friendly and traditional atmosphere. Man traps and plaques decorate the wall outside.

The Gin Trap's homecooked food is justly famous too. Specialities of the day are written up on a board and there is fresh fish on Fridays. The choice ranges through the usual pub snacks to more substantial dishes. The ham is excellent and the Narborough trout and steak and kidney pie are especially delicious. Nibbles are offered free on the bar on Sundays. Food is served every day. Meals and drinks can be taken into the attractive walled beer garden while the dining room with pew seating is a no-smoking area. Eating also takes place in the comfortable open plan bar areas on two levels. Children are only allowed on the upper level away from the bar and near to the garden. The comfortable atmosphere is emphasised by a log burner surrounded with shining toasting forks, which gives cheer during winter months.

As a freehouse the pub has Worthington and Adnams Bitter on draught as well as the Gin Trap's own brew from Woodforde's and different guest beers. Blackthorn cider is on draught too and a choice of three lagers is on offer.

At the rear is a walled garden (where dogs are allowed on leads). A converted barn on one side of the yard is a gallery which has changing exhibitions. There are lots of good walks in the area and the Peddar's Way runs through the village. Walkers are welcome. Bed and breakfast is available and the pub stays open all day in summer.

Telephone: (Holme) 01485 525264.

How to get there: Ringstead is about 2 miles off the A149 coast road signposted from Old Hunstanton.

Parking: There is a large gravelled car park to the front and more parking to the side of the pub. Cars can also be parked near the Courtyard Farm footpath (see map).

Length of the walk: Less than 4 miles of easy walking along small lanes and broad green tracks. OS Map Landranger series 132 North West Norfolk (GR 707404).

This rectangular walk contrasts the cosy and compact architecture to be seen in Ringstead village with the wide open spaces of the surrounding countryside – farmland on slopes verging on Ringstead Common not far from the coastal strip. The common was set aside at the time of Enclosure in 1781 and planted with gorse to provide fuel for the parish. There are now picnic areas which allow access to this wildlife haven. The route of the walk follows a lane with wide verges (these wide lanes could date from troop manoeuvres in Roman times or have been used as old drove roads for herding animals) and then a permissive path through Courtyard Farm whose owner Lord Melchett has a policy of farming with conservation in mind. Of interest on the walk is the wide variety of beautiful old farm buildings – some in chestnut brown local carstone, some flint and clunch, some pantiled, some slated.

The Walk

Turn left out of the pub and at a nearby T-junction turn left again along a road signposted to Docking. Walk along the pavement on the right

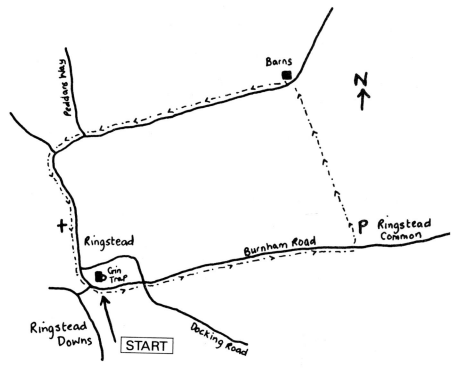

hand side of the lane with open countryside on the right. At the next
road junction you meet the Peddar's Way coming in from the right;
a historic route now designated a long distance footpath and running
from Knettishall Heath in Suffolk to meet the Norfolk Coast Path at
Holme next the Sea. Keep ahead along the Burnham road passing a
little green round a chestnut tree. Pass Foundry Lane on the left.
Continue along this wide verged road into open rolling farmland
dotted with trees and hedges. Turn round to admire the lovely view
of Ringstead church and the woods of Old Hunstanton estate beyond.
After about a mile along this quiet little road, a stony track crosses to
right and left marked by a wooden footpath signpost. Just further on
is Ringstead Common – a wild area of trees, gorse and flowers. A
detour can be made to visit this.

For the main walk turn left through a gateway along the stony track
passing a notice about Courtyard Farm circular walks. Lord Melchett,
very public spiritedly, created about 5 miles of new public footpaths
in 1982 to provide three circular walks which can also be explored.
Courtyard Farm also offers bunkhouse accommodation for 12 people.
Cars can be parked on the green verge on the right here. Continue

along the track through farmland. North Wood defines the brow of the hill over on the right. The track goes uphill with a hedge and then a narrow copse on the left. After some distance a wooden marker points the farm walk to the right. For this walk, keep on ahead here passing through wooden gates to the road. Turn left along this quiet lane passing a splendid collection of barns on the right. The road goes uphill through an avenue of old beech and oak trees, somewhat gnarled from the winds from the sea not far off over the brow of the hill on the right. Again there is a good view of Ringstead church nestling in trees over the fields ahead. On the right stands an old windmill now minus its sails.

At the road junction, carry straight on along Holme Road walking on the pavement. At the next T junction turn left and walk along the pavement into the village passing various lovely old houses and farms including Ringstead rectory in brown carstone on the right, then the flint church of St Andrew set on a hillock dominating the landscape around. This church is the remaining one of three churches in Ringstead. Built of local carstone and basically 14th century, it was restored in 1865 and has many interesting features inside. Pass the post office, shop and tearoom on the right, go over Chapel Lane and carry on to the pub.

Another interesting walk is to Ringstead Downs which are down a wide track off the Sedgeford road beyond Hall Lane. This is the site of the church of St Peter, originally the mother church in Ringstead Magna, with its round tower still standing in the grounds of Bury House, formerly the rectory. This steep chalky valley, unusual in mainly sandy Norfolk, is a Site of Special Scientific Interest and a Norfolk Wildlife Trust Nature Reserve. The path through leads to Barrett Ringstead or Ringstead Parva where the remains of Ringstead's third church, another St Andrew's, lie not far from an ancient house standing by a spring-fed pond.

Wiggenhall St Germans
The Crown and Anchor

This old Greene King pub is in a lovely position by the banks of the river Great Ouse at the east end of the bridge which links Wiggenhall St Germans and Wiggenhall St Peter with the other Wiggenhalls on the west bank – St Mary the Virgin and St Mary Magdalen. The pub is painted cream with some dark timbering and a timber porch. A large anchor lies near the river bank. The banks are high here as a protection against flooding but there are views over the river from the dining room which is up a flight of stairs from the lounge bar. You may be lucky enough to see the seal which swims up and down this reach. The lounge bar and its raised eating area are carpeted and the furnishings give an air of old fashioned comfort. There is a coal fire (in winter) in a brick fireplace enlivened by horse brasses and interesting old photographs of the pub and village hang on the wall opposite. The public bar has darts, pool table and a fruit machine and is lined with trophies from the darts and pool teams. Outside the splendid church looms over the pub. On a pleasant evening you can always sit at the tables which line the grassy bank and view the river while you drink.

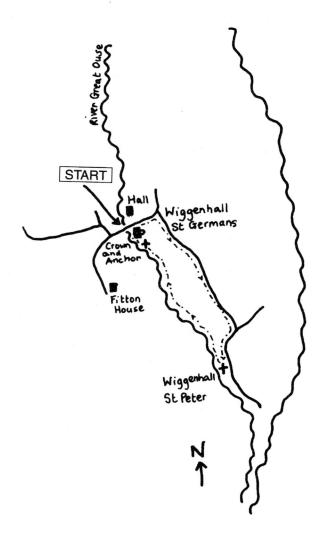

There is a range of good, home-made, reasonably priced bar food, such as steak and kidney pie. The sandwiches are excellent and meals are served every day. The beers are IPA, Ruddles Smooth, Caffreys and guest beers. Scrumpy Jack cider is on draught, together with a choice of lagers. The pub keeps usual opening hours.

Telephone: (King's Lynn) 01553 617340.

How to get there: Wiggenhall St Germans is about 5 miles south of King's Lynn and is signposted from the A47.

Parking: There is some parking in front of the pub. An alternative parking place would be by Wiggenhall St Peter church.

Length of the walk: About 2 miles of easy walking along lanes and the river bank. Be prepared for some mud here after rain. OS Maps Landranger series 131 Boston and Spalding (GR 596141) going on to 132 North West Norfolk.

Although the Wiggenhalls are fairly close to King's Lynn, they have a strange feeling of remoteness and timelessness probably caused by the fact that they are cut off by the river Ouse, the New Bedford River and the Middle Level Drain. A new channel was cut in 1953 after St Germans was badly flooded when the river bank was breached in several places. The charm of this walk lies in the views from the raised river bank across typical fenland.

The fens have a strange and particular atmosphere and are steeped in history. There is a great tradition of ecclesiastical foundations attracted by the remoteness of the marshes and each of the four villages of the Wiggenhalls has a magnificent church. This short walk links Wiggenhall St Germans and the hamlet of Wiggenhall St Peter with its romantic ruined church dominating the river. Walking along the river bank on a sunny day reveals the full extent of the waterways, drains, dikes, ditches and cuts which drain the marshy land. You can see for miles over the flat countryside punctuated by small fenland farmhouses and smallholdings, the towers and spires of churches and the massive sugar beet factory on the outskirts of King's Lynn. Dorothy L Sayers evoked the atmosphere of these fenland villages with their great churches in her detective story 'The Nine Tailors'.

The Walk

Turn right out of the pub and walk along the main road past an agricultural machinery centre, various houses and a Methodist chapel to a road junction. Turn right here, signposted to Wiggenhall St Peter, going through more housing and out into the countryside towards St Peter's church in the distance. This lane is a typical fenland lane with no hedges to hinder the wind which sweeps over the flat farmland. At a junction of lanes with a grassy triangle in the middle near a few houses, turn right down St Peters Road (No Through Road signpost) with a deep ditch on the left to the small hamlet of Wiggenhall St Peter which is little more than a farmhouse and a few ancient cottages round the ruined church standing right by the high bank of the river Ouse.

Turn right up an alley between a terrace of old cottages on the right. In one of these, an old man and his cat guard the ruined church opposite from their sunny window. Spare a moment to look at the remains of this beautiful church. Worship ceased here before the Second World War but it is now in the keeping of the Norfolk Churches Trust. The tower is 15th century, built of a mixture of brick, flint and rubble. A south aisle was demolished in Victorian times. The carved heads both inside the nave and decorating the stone windows outside are particularly appealing.

Go up the bank and turn right along it going over a stile. The river Great Ouse on the left is tidal and can be smelly at times but seems to support plenty of bird life. Continue walking along the high bank which offers wide views all round. Almost hidden by trees on the opposite bank is Fitton House, built in Tudor redbrick and said to have been an abbey before that. Further on, on the left can be seen the tower of Wiggenhall St Mary the Virgin church (the marvellous interior has carved poppy head benches of 1500, supposedly the best in England, and medieval stained glass). There is a good view of Wiggenhall St Germans church ahead near the gently curving river bridge.

Cross a stile by a gate near the church. Bear right down the bank and spend a little time looking at the church with its restored stone tower adorned with a painted wrought iron clock and a pretty porch of ancient red brick. The inside has a strong medieval feeling with richly carved 15th century benches and 17th century pulpit and furniture. Go down the alley leading to the church to reach the pub on the left. Before stopping for a drink, it is worth crossing the road and continuing along the bank for a short detour to see 17th century St Germans Hall with its little garden gazebo overlooking the river.

Wimbotsham
The Chequers

This friendly pub stands in the middle of the somewhat scattered village of Wimbotsham on the edge of a pretty green. It is a central part of village life and is much frequented by the locals, though visitors also find a warm welcome. Like so many other pubs in the region, the Chequers started life as an estate pub and it was later taken over by Greene King. The mellow brick and pantiled building is about 350 years old and inside a lovely old inglenook has been knocked through into the restaurant and makes a cheerful focal point, adorned with shining horse brasses and other brass artefacts. The pub boasts an inanimate collection of ducks to add further interest to the interior and, as in all good locals, darts and pub games are available and the pub piano can be used for sing-songs. Dogs and children are also welcome provided that their behaviour is up to scratch.

The pub keeps usual midweek opening hours and food is served every day from 12 noon to 2 pm and from 6.30 pm to 9 pm (no food on Tuesday evenings). On Saturday the pub is open all day for serving drinks while meals can be ordered from 12 noon to 2 pm and from 6.30 pm to 9.30 pm. The usual menu consists of a variety of delicious meals cooked by the landlord. Lunchtime meals include sandwiches, as well as regular specialities and the pub's famous steak and ale pie. There is a separate function room.

As a Greene King pub the main beers on draught are Greene King IPA and Abbot. Guinness and Strongbow cider are also on draught and there is a good selection of lagers.

Telephone: (Downham Market) 01366 387704.

How to get there: Wimbotsham is a mile north of Downham Market just off the A10.

Parking: There is plenty of parking space in the pub car parks at the front and back, also by the green or next to the recreation ground.

Length of the walk: About 2 miles but this can be increased by carrying on down Longchurch Lane to the New Bedford river or following other arrowed paths back to the village. OS Map Landranger series 143 Ely and Wisbech (GR 620051). There is a leaflet on walks round Wimbotsham in the Norfolk Parish Walks series published by Norfolk County Council.

Although Wimbotsham is on the edge of the fens and only a mile or so from the drainage channel of the New Bedford river, it has a character all of its own. The pretty village houses are built mainly of dark brown carstone or an unusual dark brick, and although the church of St Mary was heavily restored in Victorian times, it still has a couple of Norman doorways and a chancel arch of similar vintage while lovely carved bench ends have a very rural feel showing mainly animals, including pigs, which may have inspired the pub collection.

The walk begins at the lovely green graced with a circular seat round one of the mature trees and an interestingly carved village sign showing a Stirling bomber which was based at the neighbouring heavy bomber airfield during the war. On the other side of the green from the pub is the Victorian school with its tall bell tower. The walk leaves the village and passes through pleasantly wooded farmland mainly along old green ways. The going is flat and fairly easy but paths can be overgrown. In late summer horseradish along one of the lanes gave a sharp scent to the air, and flowers such as rose bay willow herb, yarrow, knapweed, hogweed, and ragwort made a patchwork of colour.

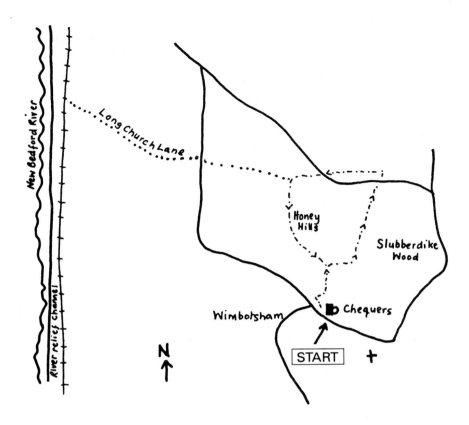

The Walk

Turn right out of the Chequers pub by the village green, and then right again by a smaller green down Miller's Lane (named after a nearby mill which was demolished in 1912), a wide muddy track bounded by a few houses. Carry on down the main track which bends to left and right. Follow it to the right where a green lane (used later) goes on ahead. Pass Rose Cottage, adorned with the date 1798, on the left and continue on. Opposite a small wooden fenced paddock, turn left along a wide grassy track leading through allotments or smallholdings. Make for a gap in the hedgerow near sheds ahead. Cross a broken stile marked with a plastic circular footpath arrow and carry on ahead along a path left through crops (the maize was head high when I walked the route). Go through a large gap in a hedgerow and continue straight on through arable land to bear right to a gateway in the right hand corner of the field (marked by a footpath signpost) near

27

interestingly named Slubberdike Woods.

Turn left along the lane here. After a short distance the lane bends to the right. At this corner go ahead onto a broad track (Longchurch Lane) by a small farmhouse on the right. Circular route markers are fixed to a post here. After a few hundred yards another track crosses.

For a longer walk you can carry straight on here for another mile or so, crossing the still used railway line carefully to reach the New Bedford river and then retracing your steps.

Turn left here (there are more arrow markers on a post) and walk along a muddy track which has a ditch and field on the left and a good view of Wimbotsham church ahead. This is called Honey Hills, perhaps because of the profusion of wild flowers attracting bees in spring and summer. Just as the track turns to gravel and houses begin, take a stile to the left and go along a narrow overgrown path fenced on the left with the garden of a bungalow on the right. Cross a stile into a meadow and continue on, keeping to the right hand edge of the meadow and passing barns on the right to reach a wooden barred gap (marked by a plastic arrow) just to the left of the field corner. Cross this and turn right down a grassy lane. This leads back onto Miller's Lane. Turn right down this to retrace your steps back to the village green and pub.

⑥ Denver Sluice
The Jenyns' Arms

The positions of the Jenyns' Arms is absolutely idyllic. It stands on the banks of the Great Ouse river with the drainage channel of the New Bedford river just beyond its car park. A feature of the pub is its terrace garden amply supplied with benches, tables and chairs for surveying the constantly changing scene – including the resident peacock. There are moorings and accommodation at the pub and the nearby basin is a collecting point for boats plying the river and cuts.

This family run freehouse was once the house of a boat builder at the turn of the century and his family photograph is one of many interesting old local photographs which hang on the walls of one of the alcoves off the main bar. This part of the building was the room of the toll collector for boat charges on the waterways and there is a list of the tolls on a board at the front of the pub. The large carpeted main bar has a brick fireplace at one end next to an antique lamp standard. A huge cast-iron bell is hung between old beams and there is another one at the other end of the bar. A conservatory along the riverfront and a restaurant/function room/pool room increase the accommodation on busy summer days. There is a fairly standard bar menu for every day and a specials board. At Sunday lunchtimes there is a popular roast; the

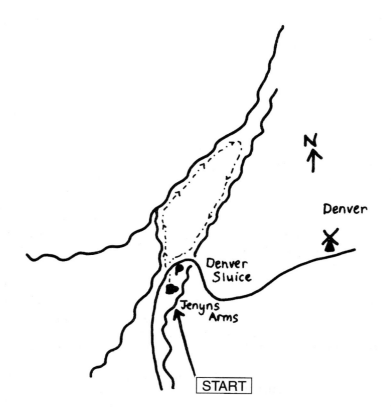

bar meals are enormous and very good value; and there are specialities each day which often consist of fresh fish. Sandwiches can be open or toasted, as well as standard. There is a good selection of lagers and beers on draught and also Scrumpy Jack and Strongbow cider. Beers include Speckled Hen, Greene King IPA, Adnams Bitter and changing guest beers.

Telephone: (Downham Market) 01366 383366.

How to get there: Denver Sluice is reached by taking a small road, signposted to Denver, off the A10 not far south of Downham Market and carrying on for a mile beyond Denver village. The Jenyns' Arms is on the same road, a little further on.

Parking: Cars can be parked at the pub or in a free public car park near the sluice. The car park has toilets, picnic tables and a slipway open to all registered boats.

Length of the walk: About 2 miles. OS Map Landranger series 143 Ely and Wisbech (GR 588009).

Denver Sluice is a very special spot and unlike any other in Norfolk, or for that matter in the whole of the Norfolk, Cambridgeshire and Lincolnshire fenland. It is the meeting place of a network of waterways, both natural and man-made, which are crucial to the management and drainage of vast areas of fenland. The whole system is a fascinating amalgam of water engineering and most of it can be seen from the walk along two raised flood banks (wrap up well on a windy day). Denver Sluice allows vessels from Peterborough travelling along the Nene to link with the river Great Ouse along which it is possible to reach Ely, Bedford and Cambridge. The river Nene also links with the Grand Union Canal. Binoculars are especially useful on this walk not only for birds but to scan the fenland countryside.

The Walk

Turn right out of the pub and follow the road round over the bridge by the sluice. At the end of the sluice turn left up a bank and over a stile onto the flood bank by the tidal river Great Ouse bearing left. Carry on over another stile and keep walking along the bank from which there are wide views over the fenland around. Over the river on the left the top floor windows of cottages peep over the defending flood bank. Lock gates at Salters Lode, the end of the Middle Level Nene-Ouse Navigation link, lead to Well Creek on the other side of the river.

Go through a gateway and keep on ahead towards Downham Market on the horizon ahead. There is a view of Denver tower windmill complete with sails over among trees on the right. The windmill was built in 1835 and was still milling corn in 1969. It was presented to the Norfolk Windmills Trust in 1971. The 14th century tower of St Mary's church, Denver, also stands out. Ahead the road bridge into Downham Market comes into sight.

Well before this as the bank begins to bear left, go to the right down the bank and take a short cut along a lower bank. Climb over a wooden barrier and continue on to meet the higher bank along the relief channel. Turn right along this broad grassy bank back towards the sluice. The patches of scrub on the sides of the bank and the reed-fringed water make excellent habitats for all kinds of water and meadow birds. I caught sight of grebes, cormorants, various ducks and quantities of swans. From here can be seen stands of poplar trees in the surrounding countryside which are planted as protection against the infamous 'fen blows' when the rich black topsoil can be blown away. Sheep, cows and horses graze the banks.

Denver Lock is the main navigation structure linking the South Level river system to the tidal river and then to the Middle Level or the sea. The Old Bedford and New Bedford rivers were dug for the Earl of Bedford by Cornelius Vermuyden, the Dutch water engineer, to shorten the passage of river water from Bedford. In addition the large area between the two rivers could store surplus flood water. He constructed the first sluice at Denver in 1651 to control tidal surges and improve navigation. It lasted into the early 18th century when it was replaced by the first navigation lock, constructed by Labelye. The present sluice and lock were designed and constructed by John Rennie in 1854 and his design remains almost intact today though various refinements have been made, including the A G Wright sluice which diverts floodwater from the river Cam and the fens into the flood relief channel which discharges at King's Lynn. This is also fed by another cut off channel which intercepts part of the flood waters from the rivers Wissey, Little Ouse and Lark. Not even a system as complex as this can cope with extreme conditions such as the combination of erosion of banks by frost, sudden thaw after heavy snow, exceptionally high tides and strong winds. Then floods occur, such as the disastrous one of 1947.

The bank becomes lower as it makes for the sluice. Carry on through a gateway and on to a metal kissing gate which leads onto the road. Turn right along the road following its bends past the public car park on the left and over the road bridge by the main sluice to reach the pub. The area is an Environment Agency water park and is very popular for water sports. There is an angling club, a sailing club, moorings for cruisers, and boats can be hired.

Narborough
The Ship Inn

The Ship Inn was once used for collecting dues and tolls from the river and the coaching route as well as for refreshment. In 1665 the pub landlord minted his own tokens for the use of bargees on the river. Here you will find a warm welcome, comfortable bars and excellent food. At one end of The Ship there is a separate locals' bar with a pool table, darts, shove halfpenny and dominoes. Entrance to the lounge bar is through a large warmly decorated lobby with some inviting seating. Off the lobby is an elegant, small dining room. To the right is the lounge bar with a red carpet, dark panelling and a painted brick fireplace which has a fire burning in cold weather. The cosy atmosphere is enhanced by magazines lying about. Well-behaved dogs are welcome. The sporting prints lining the walls indicate the special flavour of this pub which can also accommodate sporting parties in its six bedrooms. Both shooting and fly fishing can be arranged by the publicans, and the results feature strongly on the delicious menu. Coarse fishing is available locally and the trout farm opposite offers fishing on a daily basis. In Summer there are tables outside at the front or at the back by the river Nar where trout can be spotted.

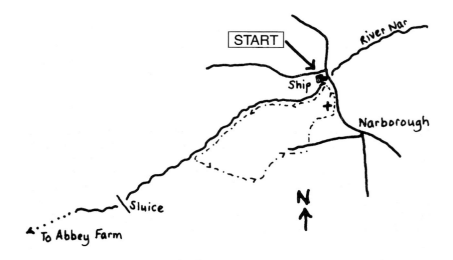

The pub has a varied bar and restaurant menu including Narborough trout as a speciality. Snacks and sandwiches are also available. No meals are served on Monday. Real ales include John Smith's as well as other guests. In the good old days the pub used to brew its own beer.

Telephone: (Narborough) 01760 337307.

How to get there: Narborough is now bypassed and the village is just off the A47 King's Lynn to Swaffham road about 10 miles from King's Lynn.

Parking: The pub has its own parking area.

Length of the walk: The walk as described is about 3½ miles but it can be extended by walking further up this delightful river bank as the right of way goes on for several miles as far as Abbey Farm. OS Map Landranger series 132 North West Norfolk (GR 745134).

The area round Narborough is a fascinating patchwork of river, lakes, beautiful houses, a mill and maltings buildings all set in woods and watermeadows. It was obviously once a centre of great activity. The river used to be navigable up to the

34

17th century and freight including coal, stone and corn was brought from King's Lynn by bargees. Flour from the mill and malt from the maltings made up the return cargo. The route of this walk is in a westerly direction along the lovely tree-lined river Nar, now a backwater full of watercress and river plants, and frequented by a variety of waterbirds including kingfishers, herons, swans, and mallards. The walk returns to Narborough through fields.

The Walk

From the pub walk a few steps to the main road and turn right along it. Cross over one branch of the river Nar which runs between the back of the pub and some huge old maltings buildings opposite a garage over the road. On the left are Narborough Trout Lakes next to the lovely old mill. Cross over a second branch of the river and turn right down a lane leading between bungalows. Bear right to a dead end by houses and look carefully for the footpath on the left which passes between high *cupressus* hedges. Follow this and bear to the right skirting a garden to reach the river bank.

Turn left at a public footpath signpost along the edge of the river on the right. When I walked, a wide path was mown all the way along the bank but it looks as if it could get overgrown at times. An odd sight was three aeroplanes standing in the field on the left. Continue on past the point where the two branches of the river join. Over the field on the right is a big willow-hung pond. Pass what is left of the old railway bridge over the river. There are houses scattered on the far bank. The river curves gently through flat farmland. Plenty of trees of varying ages and stands of poplars punctuate the peaceful scene. The path at one stage is overhung with trees on both sides. The walk reaches a bridge where it is possible to cross and return along the other bank. For a longer walk continue on ahead along the river bank to Abbey Farm but return to the concrete building described below to follow the return route as some of the other footpaths leading away from the river have disappeared.

To follow the route of this walk, retrace your footsteps at the bridge to a concrete pumping building down the bank on the right. Go down the bank (muddy at the bottom) then through an ancient metal gate to the left into a big meadow. Follow the fenced and tree-hung ditch at right angles away from the river keeping as far as possible to the boundary on the right. Cross a ditch and go into the next field, heading in the direction of a sewage works over the field. Go through metal gates to the right of the sewage works onto a broad stony track with woods on the left. Continue ahead along this track over a small stream, then go through a series of metal gates to a junction of tracks.

Turn left at a footpath signpost through the middle of an arable field, cross over a ditch into another field and bear slightly rightish across the middle of this (a clear path even when crops are sown) towards bungalows and the church. Go through a metal gate by a bungalow and along a fenced off path along gardens with a field over on the left. Go through a wooden barrier and pass between flint walls of the church (All Saints' church contains exceptional monuments and brasses to the local landowners, the Spelman family) and a lovely old farmhouse on the left to reach the main road. Turn left along the pavement, passing a sandstone chapel on the left and a lodge built from similar materials with pretty bargeboards, over the road on the right. Pass the bungalows where the outward footpath turned off and go over the two branches of the river Nar back to the pub.

To the east of the main road the river flows through the beautiful grounds of Narford Hall past a series of lakes and pools through West Acre and on to Castle Acre where the ruins of the famous priory are well worth visiting. Another walk at Narborough is along the track of the old railway through a Norfolk Wildlife Trust Nature Reserve which offers a rich variety of chalk grassland plants and a large and diverse butterfly population.

8 Colkirk
The Crown

The atmosphere at the Crown pub is friendly and comfortable. Its two attractive bars have a traditional feel, with tiled floors, pleasant rugs, some pew seating and a cheery open fire. The non-smoking restaurant is painted a lively yellow with blue and white plates on the wall – indeed blue and white china is a feature of the pub. It is open every day from 11 am to 2.30 pm and 6 pm to 11 pm (12 noon to 3 pm and 7 pm to 10.30 pm on Sundays) and food can be ordered for a reasonable period within those times. There is a patio area and garden to the rear of the pub. Children are welcome and dogs are allowed in the bar area. There is a map of local walks on the wall outside.

The choice of food is wide with home-made specials on a blackboard. Steak and ale pie is popular as is the fresh fish. There are several vegetarian options and a list of delicious puddings, as well as roasts on Sunday. Beers are Abbot IPA and XX Mild as well as guest beers. Scrumpy Jack cider is on draught.

Telephone: 01328 862172.

How to get there: Take the A1065 out of Fakenham. At Hempton turn left onto the B1146 road to Dereham. Colkirk is signposted on the right.

Parking: There is a large car park to the rear of the pub.

Length of the walk: 5 miles. OS Map Landranger series 132 North West Norfolk (GR 264921).

The combination of a good pub, a pretty village and rolling farmland makes for a very enjoyable walk. The village has no special claim to fame, though its name probably indicates the existence of an early church. The present church of St Mary the Virgin is made of rounded small cobblestones with a battlemented tower; the lovely circular font bowl is Norman. Oxwick church, passed on the walk, is a romantic ruin. Colkirk and its surrounding farmland is typical of so many in Norfolk – off the beaten track and approached down tiny lanes, set in attractive farmland punctuated by trees and copses.

The Walk

Turn left out of the pub along the pavement of Crown Road. Bear left round the corner into Church Road and continue on. At a junction of roads near the war memorial continue ahead along Church Road. Opposite the church of St Mary the Virgin, turn left down Gordon's Lane. At the next T junction turn right and walk along a bendy lane for some distance past ditches and copses. Past the drive to Field Over on the left, the road bends to the left. As it begins to bend to the right, take a signposted broad path on the left passing a dwelling called Duck Waddle Barn. Where the hard track veers sharply to the left, continue straight on along a grassy path between fields (a short section of fencing on the left to begin with). The path bends slightly right then passes to the left of a hedge with a ditch at its foot. Continue ahead past the ruins of romantic Oxwick church (All Saints, 14th century) on the right.

Avoid a bridlepath to the left and come out onto a lane on a bend. Go ahead along this lane, passing a farm with a telephone box outside on the right. Bear left with the drive to Green Farm on the right. Follow the lane to the right passing extensive buildings at Manor Farm. The lane bends to the left and then left again at Bottlebrake Farm with its interesting ponds. For a **short cut** at the next T junction, bear left and walk for some distance until the road bends left and then right on the outskirts of Colkirk. At the T junction turn right and then very shortly left and continue back to the Crown.

For the **full walk**, turn right at the T junction, and go gently uphill. At the next junction, ignore the right turn to Whissonsett and continue

38

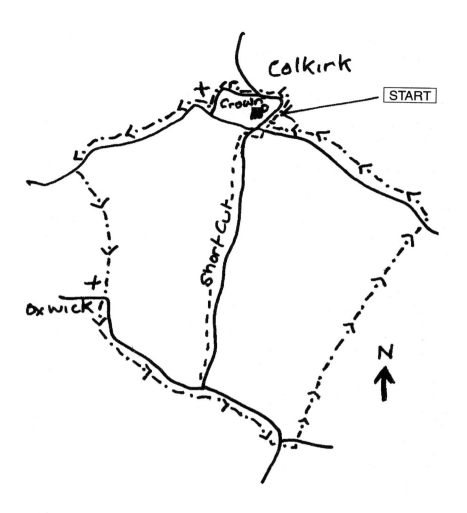

Colkirk

START

Crown

Shortcut

Oxwick

N

ahead signposted to Horningtoft. After a short distance, turn left off the lane at a field entrance (footpath signpost) and head off slightly towards the left across a large field, heading for the far corner of a hedgerow which comes part of the way down this field. Here there is an arrow marker on a post pointing the path slightly to the right, this time across an arable field, aiming for a point two thirds of the way to the right along a stand of poplars in the distance. At the next field edge and marker post, cross a little bridge and head again slightly to the left across a smaller field towards the left hand end of the stand of poplars with a farmhouse behind. Another marker post points the way onto a concrete drive. Turn left then immediately right along this, bearing left past the pond at Hazelwood Farm and continuing on along a hedged track. Pass Manor Farm on the left and come out onto Dereham Road. Turn left along the road for some distance passing houses and cottages old and new. At a road junction in the village bear right to reach the pub.

North Elmham
The King's Head Hotel

9

The king who lends his title to this inn is Henry VIII whose face stares out haughtily from the pub signpost. Hotel is a slightly exaggerated term for this pub but it does have a few bedrooms for letting, and the stained glass semicircular canopy over the door is certainly grand enough for a hotel entrance. The pub is a three storied brick and pantiled building with a large and ancient pump in one corner in front, and old stabling to the side. These are indications of the inn's long history of giving succour to travellers and their horses on this crossroads of the King's Lynn to Aylsham and Fakenham to East Dereham turnpikes just on the edge of the village. The pub has a tradition of being at the centre of local life. The hunt used to meet here regularly and the restaurant was once used as a court room for dispensing local justice.

The lobby, corridors and restaurant of the King's Head have a warm deep pink William Morris style wallpaper with other soft furnishings toning in. The restaurant is spacious, seating 40 plus with comfort, and has patio doors leading into an enclosed garden with outdoor tables and a play area where children can entertain themselves safely if they get bored with eating. There is also a small snug which can be used as a function room or as an overflow area for bar snacks. Pictures of coaching scenes and old photographs hang everywhere and the lounge bar, with its cheery open fire in winter, is graced with a collection of hats. The separate public bar has pool and darts and collections of cigarette cards on the walls.

There is an à la carte menu with a large number of starters. The main dishes include grills, vegetarian meals and a special children's menu. There is a separate bar snacks menu. Any special dishes are written up on a board and may include fresh fish or traditional stew and dumplings. At Sunday lunchtimes there is a popular carvery at a reasonable set price. The real ales in this freehouse are Greene King IPA, Woodforde's and guest beers with Dry Blackthorn cider on draught. There is also a good selection of draught and bottled lagers. Dogs are allowed in the garden and public bar.

Telephone: (North Elmham) 01362 668856.

How to get there: The King's Head is on a crossroads of the B1145 King's Lynn to Aylsham and the B1110 Holt to East Dereham roads about 5 miles from Dereham.

Parking: In the pub car park or there is limited parking near the village sign by the entrance to the Saxon cathedral on the B1110.

Length of the walk: About 3 miles along village streets, a disused railway line and a green lane. OS Map Landranger series 132 North West Norfolk (GR 984206). The Norfolk Parish Walks series of leaflets published by Norfolk County Council describes another walk in North Elmham and there is also a leaflet in the Wensum Valley Walks series which details a longer walk which goes past the restored County School station which has a visitor centre, tearoom and toilets (open at weekends).

This walk offers glimpses of the history of this important village which was once the heart of early Christianity in Norfolk. The route passes the lovely park and vineyard surrounding what was the Old Hall, the magnificent church and the fascinating remains of a Saxon cathedral and then goes along a now disused railway line which has plenty of wildlife interest. An old green lane leading from the cathedral to the river offers lovely views over the Wensum Valley to Bintree woods and Billingford Common. The route of this walk is part of a series of walks undertaken by the Wensum Valley project and there is an opportunity to explore further by studying the board by the Saxon cathedral car park which describes another loop walk to the north of the village. Not far from the village to the south is Spong Hill, site of a large Anglo-Saxon cemetery on the side of Blackwater Valley which revealed important finds, now in the Norwich Castle Museum.

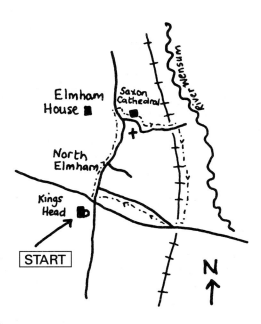

The Walk

Turn right out of the door of the pub and then left along the road signposted to Holt, which leads through the village. Cross over a road junction and continue along the main street of North Elmham walking along the pavement on the right past an interesting cross section of village houses. On the house wall to the right of the post office is an old fire insurance plaque. The parkland of Elmham House on the left was designed by Repton. The Old Hall was remodelled early in the 19th century and there are glimpses of the hexagonal brick venison and game larder and the round dovecote with its conical tiled roof and weathervane over the flint boundary wall. In the middle of the wall is an old milestone showing London 111 miles, Dereham 5 and Holt 13. A holly bounded cemetery on the right leads to Elmham's wonderful church of St Mary the Virgin which is noted for its huge late 14th century tower and vaulted porch roof. Inside is a splendid rood screen adorned with paintings of saints, carved medieval bench ends and a Jacobean pulpit and altar table. Opposite are the entrance gates to Elmham House and the pretty lodge which displays the lion crest of the Sondes family who bought the Park in the 19th century. Several village houses also carry the crest. The old stable block is now the home of Elmham wines and the vineyards can be seen in the grounds. Archaeological excavations carried out in the 60s and 70s in the Park grounds just opposite the cathedral showed Anglo-Saxon occupation and a large burial ground.

Just past the church is a small car parking area on the right by the village sign and an explanatory notice board. The Saxon cathedral (owned by English Heritage) or Bishop's chapel is to the left and is well worth a detour. In the 6th and 7th centuries, the early Christian authorities divided East Anglia into two dioceses of the North Folk and the South Folk and the northern diocese was centred on North Elmham – hence the building of the Anglo-Saxon cathedral. Later the centre of ecclesiastical power was moved to Thetford and then Norwich, and the Elmham cathedral became the precursor of the great cathedral at Norwich. Remains of a wooden Saxon cathedral have been unearthed. A later stone structure was built by Bishop de Losinga in the 11th century, but much of the stone building visible now dates from the 14th century when Bishop Despenser of Norwich converted the cathedral into a defended hunting lodge.

From the parking area, turn right down a lane passing a few houses. This turns into Church Lane, a hedged green lane (sometimes muddy in places) which winds gently towards the railway line offering lovely views over the Wensum Valley. There are occasional plastic arrow markers put up by the Wensum Valley Project. Cross a small bridge over the former railway and turn immediately left, crossing a stile and going down steps onto the old railway line. Turn left along it under the bridge. The track is stony and passes at first through a tree studded embankment then through fields edged with bracken and gorse. Cross over a slightly raised track between two fields and continue on. There is now a section of track remaining on the left hand side and more track is apparent as the line nears the village. Continue on between barns and workshops to the level crossing gates. Go through a small white gate on the right and turn immediately sharp right along Eastgate Street. The road curves round to the left and has a pavement on the right for most of its length. It goes through a section of open countryside then passes a variety of houses and cottages of different ages. Note a white cottage on the right with the Sondes family lion crest on the front. Pass a Methodist chapel on the right and come to a T junction. Turn left to reach the pub.

⑩ Great Cressingham
The Windmill

This very successful pub has been run by the same family for many years and there are memories of when the Old Bar at the end of the building was the tap room and the landlady would go down into the cellar for a jug of beer to pour out for her regulars. The Windmill is situated in a quiet country road outside the main part of Great Cressingham village a few miles south of Swaffham. It takes its name from an old cornmill nearby of which only the stump is now left. There is, however, a huge picture of the mill in all its glory on a wall inside the pub. The Old Bar (a no smoking area) is a nicely furnished room with leather armchairs either side of the 14th century fireplace over which hangs a lovely antique clock. Rather splendid Victorian pictures are on the walls. There is no separate restaurant but you can eat anywhere in the complex of friendly small rooms. An attractive conservatory leads into a pleasant garden with a play area. Everywhere are prolific tubs and pots of flowering plants. Surprisingly, an old fashioned red telephone box complete with working telephone stands inside near the loos. There is a games room with pool and darts, and private rooms are available for meetings and parties.

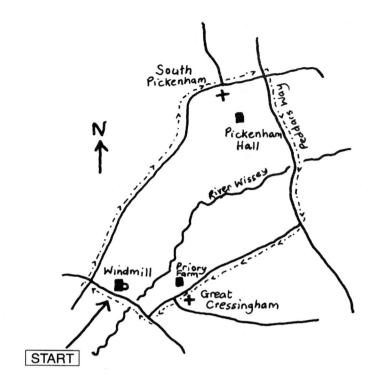

Excellent food is served every day during normal pub hours. Several separate menus combine to offer a comprehensive selection of starters, main courses and puddings, or sandwiches and snacks if those meet your requirements. There are the usual pub dishes such as scampi, lasagne and huge grills with added specialities available throughout the week. On Sundays there is a roast. Special coffees are served to round off the meal. Children have a menu all to themselves and there are several rooms in the pub which are suitable for them. You are welcome to bring your dog in provided that he is well behaved. A wide selection of well-kept beers is on offer ranging through Adnams Bitter, Broadside, Greene King IPA, Windy Miller and guest beers. Strongbow and Scrumpy Jack cider are on draught.

Telephone: (Great Cressingham) 01760 756232.

How to get there: Great Cressingham is reached by turning off the A1065 about halfway between Swaffham and Mundford. The pub is near the river Wissey just before the turning into the village.

46

Parking: There is car parking at the rear of the pub and also on a pretty tree-hung area opposite which leads to a grassy field which is available for use by Caravan Club members. You may also be able to park in the village.

Length of the walk: Just over 5 miles on small lanes with some gentle uphill walking. OS Map Landranger series 144 Thetford and Breckland (GR 845019).

This pleasant walk goes along small roads and tiny lanes through undulating farmland in the valley of the river Wissey. Higher up the slope is the beautiful park, woods and farmland of Pickenham Hall, one of Norfolk's premier shooting estates. The woodland near the hall and church is a mass of flowers in spring. The walk goes through the small village of South Pickenham to reach Peddar's Way which here follows a tiny lane through woods and farmland. A lane off Peddar's Way leads to Great Cressingham passing the moats and remains of an ancient priory, then the great church with its huge 15th century buttressed tower and glorious west doorway. A right turn leads over the river Wissey and back to the pub. There is army training land in the area and you will see notices directed at army personnel.

The Walk

Turn right out of the pub and walk along the road past Waterend Farm on the right. At the first crossroads turn right up a small road which offers lovely views over farmland in the valley of the river Wissey. Some far-sighted 19th century landowner must have planned the planting of the substantial mature trees which line this road. Pass Great Cressingham Wood over on the left, then Valley Farm on the right. The road leads on for about 1½ miles passing the unusual sight of a small vineyard on the right. The road reaches the woods of the Pickenham Hall estate on the right and then parkland dotted with trees and sheep with glimpses of the Hall beyond, rebuilt in 1904 using old materials. Pheasants strut everywhere.

Turn right at a small crossroads passing a lodge and the entrance to the Hall on the right and continue on through mature woodland containing some wonderful trees. Enchanting All Saints' church on the right is built of flint with a delicate round tower and was restored at the same time as the Hall. The romantic churchyard is surrounded by an ivy and rose hung flint wall. At a junction of roads by another Dutch gabled entrance lodge to Pickenham Hall, carry straight on along a stretch of the B1077 signposted to Ashill and Watton. Cross over the river Wissey and walk on along the road which still has woodland on either side, more recent plantations mixing in with older, mature stands.

After passing an old pond on the right, you come to a small

crossroads. Turn right here down a tiny lane which is part of Peddar's Way as the sign on the left at the crossroads indicates. This road (signposted to Great Cressingham) is little more than a farm track. It passes through lovely countryside of woods stitched together with undulating farmland crossing a tributary of the Wissey which runs through Caudle Common on the right.

After a mile or so, take a lane to the right (signposted to Great Cressingham – No entry for military vehicles) leaving Peddar's Way. Again there are good views over the Wissey valley on the right. Pass a sadly derelict farm with a medley of lovely flint outbuildings. There are glimpses of Priory Farm on the right ahead (the priory is a fine 16th century brick building incorporating earlier work) and the splendid church of Great Cressingham, St Michael's, standing high on its hillside on the left. Come down into the village past the entrance to Priory Farm. Pass the church with its carved stone tracery over the tower door on the left. The inside is huge and airy, and there are splendid carved figures on the nave roof, carved pew ends and Jacobean panelling. Some old stained glass dates back to the 15th century and there are some interesting brass memorials of the late 15th and early 16th centuries.

Bear right at a T junction and carry on downhill passing a variety of cottages and walls. Great quantities of flint are used in various ways – some rounded flint, some knapped, and some used in combination with other materials such as the flint and brick school of 1840 built for the instruction of the poor, as the tablet on the front proclaims. Turn right at a T junction and follow the road back to the pub, crossing the white-railinged bridge over the river Wissey.

Mundford
11 The Crown Hotel

The Crown Hotel, whitewashed and pantiled, with colourful window boxes, has been a hostelry since it was built in about 1650 and stands facing a small village green carefully watched over by the Victorian chapel opposite. The two sections of the Village Bar (one with a pool table) are divided by open beams of old timber and are furnished with pews and cast iron pub tables. The pub is central to village life and is the meeting place for several clubs. The Squire's Bar is hung with various pictures and notices of local interest and from this a wrought iron spiral staircase leads to the club room above where children are welcome. The Crown has over 30 bedrooms including some in the converted original coach house. As the land is higher at the back a door leads from this level to a patio area where drinks can be taken al fresco. Also upstairs is the Court restaurant and dining room for the hotel, furnished in Victorian style.

The food at the Crown is delicious and is served every day from 12 noon to 3 pm and 7 pm to 10 pm, though the pub is open all day every day. The à la carte menu for the restaurant is interesting and varied. A sample choice would be chicken etouffe, medley of local Ickburgh duck, monkfish and lobster tails, or broccoli, Stilton and oyster mushroom tart. The bar menu is excellent and reasonably priced with fish taking a leading role and some interesting vegetarian dishes. There are special roasts on Sundays. The choice of salads is extensive and a variety of vegetables is served. As a free house, the Crown offers Woodforde's prize-winning range of real ales including Wherry, and also the local Iceni ales and Courage Directors. Strongbow cider is on draught and there is a good selection of lagers. French house wines are specially selected and shipped for the Crown. Smokers are looked after by the provision of an ash rack; if you want to smoke you must help yourself to an ashtray.

This famous sporting inn of Breckland was visited by many well-known people. The 'Squire of all England', George Osbaldeston, took refreshment at the bar during a shoot when the party included the Duke of Rutland and the bag was 309 pheasants, 7 woodcock and 62 rabbits. As befits a sporting pub dogs are welcome. One of the oldest houses in the village, the inn was built by the then owners of nearby Lynford Hall although an earlier hostelry stood on the site – part of the lands of the Duke of Norfolk which reverted to the Crown on his conviction for treason, hence the name of the hotel. The inn belonged to the sporting estate until 1924, and it was run by the family of its previous owners for three generations. The present dining room was once the Court Room for the local magistrates and in use for dispensing local justice from 1655 to 1925.

Telephone: (Thetford) 01842 878233.

How to get there: The A134 and the A1065 cross at a roundabout just south of Mundford in Breckland. The pub is down a short turn off the A1065.

Parking: There is parking outside the pub and around the village green. Alternatively cars can be parked by Lynford Arboretum.

Length of the walk: 3 ½ miles of fairly easy walking. OS Map Landranger series 144 Thetford and Breckland (GR 804938).

This walk is a happy example of an excellent pub coinciding with a really beautiful route. The inn has something of the atmosphere of a French country restaurant and the forest glades also give you the impression that you could be in the French countryside. Thetford Forest covers about 80 square miles and is the second largest forest in England. In this section, apart from lovely woodland, there are added bonuses along the route. You can branch off to visit Lynford Arboretum (dogs not allowed) which is a collection of hundreds of species of conifers and broadleaved trees, the first plantings being made in 1947 by forestry students amongst the mature trees of the

50

Lynford Hall woodland. There is also Lynford Lake, a long sliver of gleaming cool green, mirroring the surrounding forest trees and offering an additional habitat to the woodland wildlife. The forest is home to a wide variety of birds, notably crossbills and red-backed shrike, and the screeching of jays can be startling. There are also some red squirrels and several varieties of deer. Other walks both long and short in this part of Thetford Forest are indicated on Forestry Commission information boards in the area.

The Walk

Turn right out of the pub and walk down Crown Road which curves a little to the left and right to meet the main road. Turn left along the main road for a short distance.

Cross carefully and go right down the lane which leads to Lynford Hall and Arboretum. After passing houses and cottages, the lane goes through a typical Breckland scene of mixed and conifer woodland all belonging to the Forestry Commission. The smell of the pine trees is magic. Walk along a gravelled path on the right hand side then a wide grass verge. Pass a gatehouse, Lynford Lodge, and the entrance to the Lynford Hall estate marked by imposing gate posts. Continue on along the lane with the stone capped pierced brick wall of the estate on the

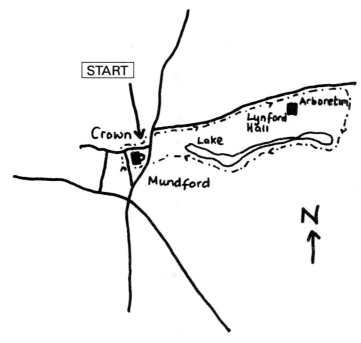

right. There are some magnificent specimen trees in the parkland beyond. Pass Lynford Hall itself – an amazing collection of red brick buildings with slate roofs, stone dressings and decorative stone work, now a Forest Hotel and Country Club with a mobile home retirement park in the grounds.

Turn right by a sign for Lynford Arboretum and walk down a broad ride next to the forest passing a parkland area and picnic tables on the right. The wooden posts with a red band on top show the route of a Forestry Commission trail. Pass a brick shelter on the left and cross the two bridges over the end of Lynford Lake.

Turn right along the lakeside and follow the broad path which curves to follow the contours of this long stretch of water. The wild flowers in this area are abundant. In late summer when I walked there were the pinks of hemp agrimony and various willowherbs, the purples of loosestrife, knapweed, and water mint and the creamy froth of meadowsweet. From the banks of the lake there are lovely views of the front of Lynford Hall. A little further on there is a rustic fishing lodge on the opposite bank.

Cross over a driveway leading to a bridge on the right and continue by the edge of the water along a broad green path with woods all around. There are now green banded posts indicating another Forestry Commission route. On the left is a huge wooden axe sculpture lying by the track. Pass a seat and carry on to the end of the lake. Just before a blue topped post turn left onto a broad grassy ride, and go through a metal barrier.

Bear right by a horseshoe marker denoting a bridleway, then ignore the broad bridleway and take a narrow green path to the right of it which passes some cottages on the left. Follow the path as it curves gently through the wood – be prepared for nettles in summer. The path broadens and comes out onto more open ground. Continue ahead down the edge of a narrow field on the right and a plantation of young conifers on the left. The houses of Mundford come into view. Cross a stile ahead into a rough field, with a mown path through it when I walked. Carry on and then go over a stile by a metal gate (wooden footpath signpost just here) which leads onto the busy main road. Cross carefully and walk on down a stony byroad (Little London Lane) lined with houses and cottages to meet a metalled road at a corner. This is Crown Road again. Go ahead up the road to reach the Crown Hotel and the green.

⑫ Thompson
The Chequers

A knight on his charger carrying a chequered shield marks the drive in to this lovely old pub which is tucked away behind a cottage along a lonely lane. The building is long, low and thatched, standing in a tree hung gravelled yard. There are benches outside at the front and a garden with tables overlooking fields at the back. The pub dates back to 1500 and was once three small dwellings, the ale house being in the middle with a cottage either side. It was owned by the Merton Hall estate until the early 1900s. Thanks to its warm welcome and excellent food and beer, it is a thriving concern.

Inside, the decor is traditional, in keeping with the original low beams, exposed brickwork and inglenook fireplace. There is one non-smoking restaurant, one smoking restaurant and one small bar (seating room for 60 people). Children are welcome in every room. Dogs can be taken into the bar and garden. The toilets include one big enough for a wheelchair.

The owner is also the head chef so food is very important. There is a bar snack menu, an à la carte menu and an ever changing daily specials board using local and seasonal products. Vegetarian meals

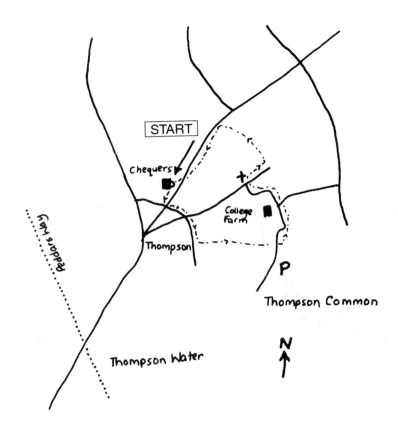

feature strongly as well as a wide variety of fresh fish. The range of real ales includes Fuller's London Pride, Adnams and Wolf.

Telephone: (Caston) 01953 483360.

How to get there: Thompson is south of Watton in Breckland and can be reached from a turning off the A1075. The pub is just outside the village on the Griston road.

Parking: The pub has a large car park. There is also parking down Butter's Hall Lane for visiting Thompson Common which is near the route of this walk.

Length of the walk: About 3½ miles, much of it over arable land. Although in summer crops may obscure the line of the path, the general route is quite obvious. Large areas of Breckland, including Stanford Training Area near Thompson, are used for army training and any no entry notices should be heeded. OS Map Landranger series 144 Thetford and Breckland (GR 922969).

This route takes you over farmland and along quiet lanes, and passes the site of the 14th century Thompson College. It follows the tree-lined river Wissey for a short distance and the road back to the pub shows you Norfolk countryside at its best — farmed fields well studded with trees and hedges and a great church providing a focal point.

The Walk

Turn right out of the pub and walk down the lane, passing some modern houses on the right just before a crossroads. At the crossroads turn left noting the splendid carved wood village sign near the junction (showing travellers on Peddar's Way, a pilgrim, a goose girl and a Roman soldier). Pass Thompson primary school on the right.

At a road junction by a grassy triangle turn right and leaving the road, go ahead down a wide tree-lined track. This passes a cottage called Pheasant View on the left and opens out into a field, continuing on with a tree-studded boundary on the right offering pleasant views over the surrounding countryside. Turn left at the end of the field, just beyond a massive oak tree, along another wide track with a wooden footpath signpost in the hedge. Follow this track down the edge of a ploughed field on the right with a hedge on the left. The hedgerow disappears in places and the track when I walked was partially ploughed up, but essentially the route continues straight ahead following the line of the hedge. When the hedge ends a footpath signpost points ahead. Follow this line to a cedarwood bungalow and garden ahead. Skirt round the garden to the right to a hedge and follow this right again (a painted sign points the way) to come through a gap onto a tiny lane.

Turn left along the lane past a cottage on the right and the bungalow and then Rose Cottage on the left. The lane bears to the right where there is a Great Eastern Pingo Trail arrow on the right. Thompson Common, to the south, is a designated Nature Reserve (grazed by Shetland ponies) run by the Norfolk Wildlife Trust. The common is noted for its pingos, circular ponds formed by Ice Age glacial action which support an interesting variety of water plants and life. They have lent their name to the Trail, a designated walk which goes through this fascinating territory. The lane crosses the river Wissey, here a small stream, and bears left. At a road junction ignore the turn signposted to Stow Bedon, and bear left down the road signposted to Thompson. Hidden in trees to the left of the lane is College Farm, the site where 14th century Thompson College (linked to the church) was founded. In the course of its restoration to a house, some interesting medieval architecture including some 14th century windows were revealed.

Turning left again at the next little junction by a post box, go over a small bridge towards the tiny triangle of College Green and some pretty cottages. College Farm is now to the left. Turn right, then turn left onto a bigger lane following it round to the right passing a lovely old barn. St Martin's church comes into view. This large and very splendid 14th century collegiate church is built of knapped flint. Inside are part of a 14th century screen and much carved Jacobean woodwork. Thompson College was founded in 1349 by the Shardelowe family with a master and five priests who served the chantry chapel of St Martin.

At a junction of lanes opposite the church, turn right along a no through road marked 'Out of Bounds to Troops'. Beyond houses on the right the road turns into a green lane. Carry on ahead along this tree hung lane to a T junction of green lanes. Turn left here onto another lane sometimes overgrown. A lovely mixture of ancient trees line this almost hidden path which looks down onto tree-studded rough land bordering the little river Wissey. The track comes out onto a small road.

Turn left along this pleasant road shaded with trees and enjoy the view of the church over the fields on the left – a typical Norfolk country scene. The lane eventually leads back to the pub.

13 New Buckenham
The King's Head

The King's Head, comfortable and traditional, was built in the 1600s and became a drover's pub linked with the extensive commons to the east of the village in 1761. It overlooks New Buckenham's pretty village green, once the site of a regular market, and the 16th century Market House raised on columns in 1745. The carpeted area of the bar opens onto a larger room with a pleasant floor of old stone and brick. Tables stand outside at the side in a paved yard hung in summer with flowering baskets. Children are welcome inside the pub. There is a wooden ramp to allow access for disabled people.

The pub is a freehouse. It offers several real ales including Adnams bitter and a variety of guest beers. Scrumpy Jack is the draught cider. It keeps usual pub hours except for the May Day and August bank holidays when it is open all day to coincide with village fairs. Food is available every day except Mondays and can be ordered up to two hours before the final bell. The dishes are home-made and freshly cooked with the accent on traditional pub food including a Sunday roast. There are several vegetarian alternatives.

Telephone: (Attleborough) 01953 860487.

How to get there: New Buckenham is about 5 miles south of Attleborough. From the A11 take the B1077, then turn onto the B1113 for a short way to reach the village and the King's Head in the Market Place.

Parking: The pub has no car park, but cars can be left adjacent to the green in Market Place.

Length of the walk: About 5 miles. OS Map Landranger series 144 Thetford and Breckland (GR 088905).

New Buckenham is a fascinating and rare example of a planned town of the 12th century. There was originally a Saxon castle at nearby Old Buckenham which was given to the Augustinians as the foundation of a priory. The Norman lord of the manor, William d'Albini, then built a new castle in 1145-50 in a better location and the village of New Buckenham was built nearby with a market to finance the castle. The streets are laid out in a grid pattern and many old and interesting buildings can be seen on the walk.

The route goes along tiny country lanes and down a right of way through a stud farm to reach the village of Old Buckenham with its huge green and lovely old church. The walk then returns along minor roads to New Buckenham castle following the line of the moat from which some romantic castle ruins can be seen. The path comes out near St Mary's chapel dating back to the 12th century which was incorporated into barns in the mid 16th century, and returns through the village to the pub.

The Walk
Turn left out of the pub and go over the crossroads down Church Street past Pump Court on the left and 13th century St Martin's church on the right. The latter is well worth a visit. Inside are three carved Elizabethan sillboards taken from a window of the Crown Inn in the Market Place and lovely stone figures of saints and angels on the nave walls. Continue on past Rosemary Lane on the left and then St Martin's Gardens, a road of new houses also on the left.

A lane goes off to the right but continue on ahead up a tiny lane passing the graveyard on the right. There are views over flat Norfolk farmland punctuated with plenty of trees. Pass Hunt's Farm on the left and then a pumping station. A footpath cutting the corner off here has disappeared so carry on along the lane which winds gently through fields on either side. Just before the road makes a determined turn to the right is a left turn marked by a grassy triangle. Turn along this. Pass a modern house on the right and the Old Hall and farm on the left.

58

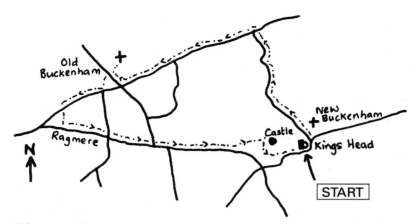

The road bends sharply to the left a little way past the Old Hall. Walk on to a green ride just here and go ahead through a white gate continuing on down a broad grassy track with a hedge on the left and a fenced field on the right. This is part of Old Buckenham Stud but don't be put off by its look of privacy – there is a public right of way through here. Continue onto a metalled drive with the gates to a house on the left. Further on pass a bungalow on the right and go through a white wooden gate to the road. There is a public footpath signpost on the right pointing back.

Come out onto Cake Street, Old Buckenham, bordering the huge village green (a registered common of 49 acres). Turn right and continue on along the main road. Opposite the war memorial on the left, a slip road to the right bears round to a lane leading right to the lovely old cream washed thatched All Saints' church with its 13th century octagonal tower and Norman archway. Leave the church by the main gate. To the right is a pub called the Ox and Plough and picnic tables on the green. Turn left to the war memorial again and turn right along the small road there which cuts through the green.

Turn right opposite Crown Road, pass Mill Farm with its pond, avoid the next right turn going round the green and continue ahead along Mill Road passing converted buildings associated with the old mill, the base of which still stands on the left. Built in 1818, it was unusually large, having five working stones instead of two or three. Shortly after this turn left down a broad track off the road with a field on the left and a hedge on the right. The woods of Old Buckenham Hall lie ahead. The track reaches another small road.

Turn left along this passing a wood on the left and scattered dwellings. Go straight over at a crossroads (Ragmere Road) again passing a scattering of houses and cottages. Carry on to a more main road which comes in from the left. Ignore a right turn and keep on along the main road passing Buckenham House on the left. Just opposite a red brick cottage sideways on to the road turn left onto the start of a stony drive to a bungalow and go over wooden bars (stile missing) which are immediately on the right with a leaning footpath signpost in the hedge and a plastic arrow marker. Walk along the fence on the left and then come onto the track. As it passes through a hedgerow, bear right through the middle of a small field with farm buildings on the left. Go through a gateway and continue straight ahead towards the church tower. Go through another gateway climbing over metal barriers (possibly a temporary structure) into a hedged section of green lane. After a short distance go through a wooden kissing gate to the left of another barrier (footpath signpost) and come out onto a broad swathe of grass surrounding the wooded moat and earthworks of the castle.

Bear right here to meet the moat, keeping it on the left and following it along going through a gateway and along a broad track passing the 19th century red brick moat bridge (incorporating parts of a 13th century gatehouse) on the left beyond which can be seen glimpses of the round flint castle keep, one of the largest and earliest in England. The path over the bridge is blocked by a wrought-iron gate. The castle is in private hands but can be visited on payment of a fee at the Castle Hill garage which you will pass further on in the walk. Continue on along the track to St Mary's chapel which still retains its Norman arches, passing it on the left to reach the road. Turn left up the pavement passing Castle Hill garage and then Dutch gabled almshouses on the right. Turn left opposite these and follow the road round to the right by the village pump near the 1884 Methodist chapel. Pass Rosemary Lane and the George pub and turn right, back to the King's Head.

There is a Village Trail (leaflets obtainable from the shop), details of which are displayed on a board under the Market House. To the east of the village lies one of the largest commons in Norfolk where grazing rights still exist and a pinder is appointed to look after the animals. There is also a wildlife area here managed by the Norfolk Wildlife Trust. It has never been ploughed and is still grazed so that traditional plants like the rare green winged orchid thrive. The Upper Tass Valley walk which runs to Hethersett starts in New Buckenham.

⒁ Garboldisham
The Fox

Though near a busy road, this useful pub is set on the edge of Thetford Forest Park and is only 2 miles from Peddar's Way which begins at nearby Knettishall Heath. It has been an inn for three centuries and was a popular stop for stagecoaches. Under a mellow pantiled roof its cream washed exterior, flower-hung for much of the year, is welcoming, and inside the traditional atmosphere is maintained with some quarry tiled floors and timber stud work. The open bar areas are divided into bays warmed when necessary by a large wood burning stove. There is a large garden with picnic tables for eating out in summer and this can be reached through the pub's conservatory. There is also a games/children's room, a no smoking lounge, and dogs are welcome.

A good range of food is usually available from sandwiches and snacks to more substantial meals. The restaurant is non smoking. Several real ales are on offer and vary but usually include Adnams bitter. There is a selection of lagers and Strongbow cider.

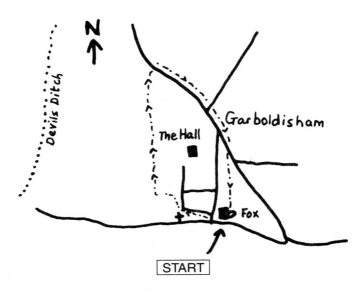

START

Telephone: (Garboldisham) 01953 688151.

How to get there: The Fox is in the village at the crossroads of the main A1066 road with the B1114 midway between Thetford and Diss.

Parking: The pub has three car parks and cars can also be parked by the green opposite.

Length of the walk: 2 miles of easy walking. OS Map Landranger series 144 Thetford and Breckland (GR 007817).

This short walk through the typical Breckland village of Garboldisham and its surrounding estate land introduces the walker to the charms of Breckland without going into the forest itself. The sandy, infertile wastes known as Breckland used to be used for little more than the cultivation of rabbits for the pot. In the late 19th and early 20th centuries, new techniques in agriculture allowed some cultivation, and forestry flourished when coniferous trees were introduced. The route of the walk passes the church of St John the Baptist with its mid 15th century tower and 13th century bell in the porch, and then the ruins of a second church standing in a field behind nearby cottages. To the west lies the Devil's Ditch, a Saxon earthwork designed to block the Roman road (now the A1066), bordering the woods of East Harling Heath. The walk goes along an old track at the back of the parkland of the Hall returning to the pub via small roads and a green lane.

The Walk

Cross over the side road outside the main door of the pub and go down Church Road opposite passing the war memorial on the left. Some nice old cottages including one with a sun dial on its wall lead on to the church of St John the Baptist on the left. Turn right at a grassy triangle at a junction of lanes walking up Back Street and passing Water Lane on the right. The ruins of Garboldisham's second church rise behind houses on the right.

Just past some bungalows on the left take an unmarked sandy track to the left with a hedge on the right and an open field on the left and make for woods ahead. At the woods turn right along a crosstrack passing an Environment Agency installation behind fencing on the left. Soon the woods on the left end and a track turns to the left, but ignore this and carry straight on.

The left hand turn should lead to the line of the Devil's Ditch beyond the belt of trees over the field on the left but sadly it petered out and was ploughed up when I walked. There are some Bronze Age barrows between the Devil's Ditch and the village.

Go along the path ahead for some distance following a small belt of trees which then becomes a hedgerow on the right studded at intervals with tall poplars and ancient oaks. From this pretty track there are pleasant views over the parkland of Garboldisham Hall hidden among the distant trees.

When eventually the track reaches a road after another belt of trees, turn right near Hall Farm and walk carefully along the road (B1111). The views from here over copses and fields studded with trees and ponds are very pleasant. Ignore the road junction on the left by the imposing gates to Garboldisham Manor and continue along the main road which is bordered on the left by the splendid red and yellow brick wall of the Manor. Pass the Old School and the Old Forge on the left and bear left up a tiny lane leaving the main road.

Follow this leafy lane gently uphill and when it veers sharply to the left, bear right up a stony track towards houses. Bear right down the side of a cottage on the left ignoring the bridleway which is signposted on the left. Then bear rightish down a pathway, passing a cottage on the left, and walk along this broad green track along the banked edge of a field on the left and the hedged and wooded grounds of a house on the right. Carry on through fields down towards the main A1066 road. At the main road turn right for a very short distance along the grassy verge to reach the pub again.

The village is near a river valley in which are the sources of the river Little Ouse and the river Waveney, the border between Norfolk and Suffolk. Various woods and heaths (including Knettishall Country Park where Peddar's Way Long Distance Path starts) and Thetford Forest, the jewel of Breckland, are close by and offer a variety of lovely wooded walks.

⑮ Pulham Market
The Crown Inn

The Crown Inn is in a prominent position in the village of Pulham Market where the main road through the village curves round the village green. It has been refreshing travellers on this route for centuries – the building is at least 400 years old. Its colourwash and thatch (complete with straw animals on the ridge) are complemented whenever possible by overflowing tubs and hanging baskets and a pretty patch of front garden. Inside the feel of an old inn has been retained, helped by quantities of old beams, an ancient inglenook, with an open fire on cold days, and walls lined with coaching prints and antique pictures. The main bar opens through to a small no smoking area with a wooden floor. The Sceptre Bar is a public bar cum games room. There is a separate restaurant open only at weekends.

Food plays an important part in the life of the Crown and meals are served at lunchtimes and in the evenings every day. Even the bread is homemade. The menu is à la carte with changing specials written up on a board. Vegetarians and vegans are well catered for. Local game in season is popular and a variety of interesting fish is a feature. Puddings tend to be traditional and delicious.

The Crown offers a varied range of real ales and Strongbow cider is on draught. The pub keeps normal opening hours and children are welcomed. There is a garden and a few benches at the front of the pub.
Telephone: (Pulham Market) 01379 676652.

How to get there: Pulham Market is about 10 miles north east of Diss and is on the B1134, just off the A140 Norwich to Ipswich road, south of Long Stratton.

Parking: There is parking to either side of the pub or next to the green at Pulham Market.

Length of the walk: About 4 miles of mainly easy walking. OS Map Landranger series 156 Saxmundham (GR 198861).

This country walk begins on the pretty green surrounded by colourwashed houses at Pulham Market. The village takes its name from its one time regular market but it was formerly known as Pulham St Mary Magdelene, while its neighbouring village was St Mary the Virgin. Many other twin villages in Norfolk once had or still have these two suffixes. The walk leaves the village and continues along the tiny lanes through undulating and most attractive farmland to reach Pulham St Mary — a village surrounded by trees. Here the church is well worth a visit before turning downhill towards the track of an old railway. It would be simple if it were possible to walk along this back to Pulham Market but it is not a public right of way. The designated footpath goes instead through some meadows, crosses a stream and continues on along the edge of a field and copse back to Pulham Market. The general direction is fairly obvious even if the actual path is not. The route of a village walk (leaflet available) comes through here too. The very slight risk of getting lost only adds to the rural charms of this walk.

The Walk

Leave the Crown and ignoring the lane to the left walk ahead up the road alongside the village green passing the post office on the left and the Falcon pub on the right. Continue on a little way and then turn right into Bank Street passing a shop on the corner. Continue along this lane out into the countryside and keep following it when it bears sharply to the left continuing downhill for some distance. There are attractive views over undulating farmland. Then the lane bends sharply to the right and goes uphill. Pass a cottage on the left and go on to a road junction.

66

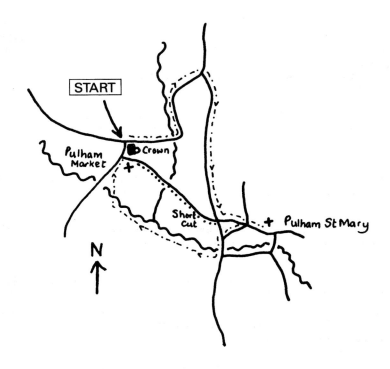

Turn right along the lane signposted to Pulham St Mary, passing Hill Farm on the right and several ponds. Further on there are good views over the countryside to Pulham Market and its church away to the right, and to the spire of Pulham St Mary church ahead on the left. Note the interesting small red barn in the field on the right. Carry on towards Pulham St Mary ignoring a turning to the left near the rather derelict looking Hill Farm (confusingly the second one on this road) on the left. Continue down the lane passing bungalows and houses to the main road (B1134) passing through Pulham St Mary. For a short cut you can turn right here and walk along a pavement all the way back to Pulham Market but this is not as interesting as the alternative route which involves a certain amount of orienteering near the old railway line.

To carry on the main walk, turn left and walk down a pavement on the right past village houses to reach the green and the King's Head pub (another good place for refreshment) on a crossroads. This old pub has 12th century beams and doors made of wood from a medieval ship. Continue on over the crossroads for a detour to visit the beautiful 15th century church of St Mary the Virgin. In late Victorian times G.F. Bodley restored the church and his screen, font and organ case are noteworthy. The magnificent south porch has a carved Annunciation and angels with musical instruments.

Return to the King's Head. On the green opposite is the village sign depicting an airship, a reminder of the nearby wartime airfield from which the airships known as Pulham Pigs flew. Turn left down Station Road passing old cottages and the former maltings on the left. Carry on downhill through new housing without turning off. Pass the junction with Mill Lane on the right and cross the road bridge over a stream. Nearly opposite where the road bends to the left, turn right along a farm track between a copse and a field passing a modern house on the right. Go along a short overgrown stretch of fenced off path to the left of metal gates. Cross a stile and continue on to a gate. Go through this into a meadow. This is where map reading skills come in useful. The public footpath should go ahead through the middle of fields, roughly following the track of the fenced off dismantled railway some yards over to the left. Go through the middle of the meadow towards a gap in the hedge on the far side. Here various pieces of hedge and gap meet but continue into the next meadow keeping along the right hand edge. Just further over is what appears to be the remnants of a green lane which is where the footpath should run. At the end of this field is a stile. Cross this and go ahead over a ditch into an arable field, turning right round the edge of this, following along the pretty stream on the right. Continue on for some distance.

At the end of the field go over a small bridge over a ditch, bear right and go over a larger bridge into a small plantation. Go left along the edge of a ditch or stream with an open field on the right. Follow the field edge along towards a new copse and houses beyond. The public footpath should go through the copse to reach the road but it was very overgrown and full of pheasants when I walked so I followed the edge of the field round to reach the road. Turn right up the road back to the Crown Inn.

⑯ Framingham Earl
The Gull

The Gull, painted pale cream with a pantiled roof, is a substantial and pleasant looking building. It is bang on the main A146 road not far from Norwich and catches passing trade as well as being the local for the scattered villages of Framingham Earl and Framingham Pigot in the peaceful countryside on the other side of the road.

The bars have a warm and cosy look with velvet curtains and dark wainscot panelling. In cold weather fires are lit in the old brick fireplace. On the walls are pictures and brass bric-a-brac. The restaurant at one end is a no-smoking area and has a Victorian cast iron fireplace. Food is served every day and the menu features traditional English food with continental specialities, and a selection of vegetarian meals and snacks. It is known for its fresh fish. The pub is freehold and offers Greene King, Abbott, Adnam's and guest beers.

Usual pub opening times are kept and meals are served within those times but the landlord will vary the hours by prior arrangement. There is no family room but a pool room down steps at the side entrance to the pub is separate from the bar area and tables are set out in summer on a grassy area up steps at the back.

Telephone: (Framingham Earl) 01508 492039.

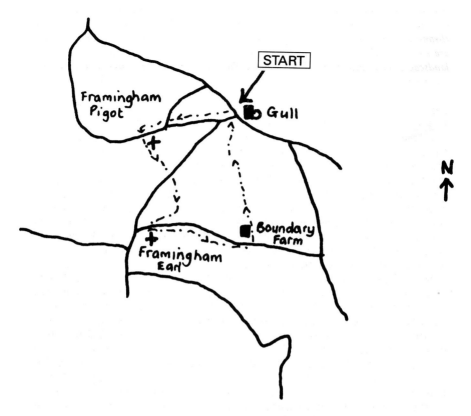

How to get there: The Gull is on the A146 Norwich to Beccles road. It is south east of Norwich and almost halfway to Loddon. Buses stop outside.

Parking: There is a good car park to the side of the Gull or cars can be carefully parked in the vicinity of the Framingham Pigot and Framingham Earl churches.

Length of the walk: Under 4 miles. OS Map Landranger series 134 Norwich and the Broads (GR 286038).

Although they are only a few miles south east of Norwich and close to the busy A146, the villages of Framingham Pigot and Framingham Earl feel as if they are lost in the heart of the countryside and are in a time warp. This is because the landscape is mainly made up of well cared for estates with small fields and streams stitched together with hedges and patches of mixed woodland. The undulating countryside encourages game birds and is stiff with pheasants and partridges, while mallards throng the ponds and boggy valleys. The two beautiful churches seen from the walk are somewhat divorced from their villages, standing out as focal points in the rural landscape. The walk skirts Framingham Pigot and returns through fields on the outskirts of Framingham Earl.

The Walk

Leave the pub and cross the busy road carefully, carrying on down a lane ahead passing houses. At a junction of roads, turn right down Chapel Lane, signposted to Framingham Pigot ½ mile. The slim minaret-like tower of Framingham Pigot church rises over the field on the left. Pass a cottage set back from the road. There is a ditch on the left of this gently curving lane. The glasshouse and plastic tunnels of a nursery and garden centre approached from the main road can be seen on the right. Pass Scatterbrook Cottage all on its own. Then, on the right, is an interesting white half-timbered house on a brick base with lovely finials at the corners of the roof. Pass this to reach a road junction and turn left to the church.

St Andrew's church at Framingham Pigot has a most unusual flint and stone conical tower graced with a fancy blue enamelled clock, and is approached through lovely flower-bedecked wrought iron gates. This High Victorian church built in 1859 replaced a Saxon one and inside is a Norman piscina and interesting Victorian fittings. Just beyond the church, turn left along a broad track (footpath signpost in the hedgerow). Then turn off the track which leads on to a house, by another footpath sign at the end of a fence. Bear left slightly and skirt round a wood behind the pink washed cottage on the right. The field is dotted with clumps of trees on the left. A stream comes in on the right and the path carries on over this and continues ahead. Pass a barn on the right. Soon a stile on the right leads into the woods. Continue on along the well marked path just inside the woods passing a large swampy pond on the right, and hedgerow trees on the left. The wood ends and the path continues on ahead through an avenue of huge old trees, eventually leaving these and continuing ahead to a stile leading onto Gull Lane.

Turn right up Gull Lane for a short way, then left at another wooden signpost across a plank bridge crossing a stream, and continue ahead along the edge of a field by a hedgerow, with trees and a ditch on the left. This path comes out onto a lane at a public footpath signpost.

A short detour to the right brings you to Framingham Earl church which is well worth a look. Another St Andrew's, it is mainly Saxon and has a characteristic round tower and early nave and chancel with circular windows. The Norman period is represented by two doorways and a chancel arch. There are also interesting monuments and some 15th century glass.

For the main walk, turn left down the lane here and walk gently downhill with a hedge on the left and a tangled wood mixed with holly and evergreens on the right. Some nice old wrought iron gates are tangled up in the boundary vegetation. The lane widens out with broad verges and some young trees planted on the right. Pass semi-detached cottages on the left and the drive leading to Church Farm on the right. After the old barns of Boundary Farm, there is a wooden footpath signpost on the verge on the right. Turn left here through the farmyard of Boundary Farm between farm buildings. The red brick farmhouse is over on the right. Also on the right is a huge pond, home to a mass of ducks, and then a smaller pond on the left. The track here can be extremely muddy and churned up by the cattle which are moved up and down. Wide and much used, it passes through a more open grassy area with old straw stacks, farm machinery and a cattle watering trough at the sides. Beyond are hedges on either side. The track goes through metal gates with an old stile to the right, and carries on as a more grassy but still wide track between hedges. There are excellent rural views of Framingham Pigot church over on the left amid a patchwork of fields and mature trees. Carry on to a public footpath signpost.

One track goes off to the right, one goes straight on, but the route of this walk goes off to the left skirting round a pond. From here you can see the main road and the Gull pub down in the valley. The track here can be very overgrown and rutted. It skirts round the edge of a field on the right with a small ditch and a bank on the left with the odd tree in it. At a hedgerow a wooden signpost points to the right. Follow this and skirt along the ancient hedge on the left (this marks the parish boundary), making for the road. Pass alongside the garden of a bungalow on the left and an open field on the right. The track comes onto a lane leading to the bungalow. Continue on alongside the boundary of another garden on the left with a copse and fields on the right and some young trees. Pass to one side of a farm gate and cross a stream just before the busy road. Turn right for a short way and cross carefully back to the pub.

Ringland
The Swan Inn

The Swan is in a lovely position on a quiet road junction near a bridge over the river Wensum. A notice warns 'weak bridge' and gives weight restrictions. The pub windows overlook watermeadows which run down to the river – a lovely place for family picnics with possibilities for fishing, and other river sports. The area has a feeling of remoteness although it is only a mile or so from the outskirts of Norwich. Inside the bar is large and L-shaped with carpet and wooden panelling. There are modern round tables and wheelback chairs in dark stained wood. On the wall is a huge $6\frac{1}{4}$ lb trout in a case, caught on Whit Monday in 1960 to prove that good fish can be taken on the river.

This is very much a local pub. It specialises in traditional English food served in its conservatory/restaurant. No food is served in the evenings at the moment. The pub is a freehouse and has on draught four real ales including Adnams Bitter. Guinness and Strongbow cider are also on draught. Although there is no family room children are welcomed and there is a garden. Dogs must wait outside the pub.

Telephone: (Norwich) 01603 868214.

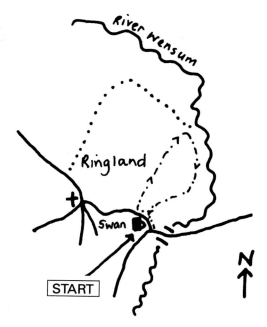

How to get there: To reach Ringland follow the signs for about 2 miles from the village of Taverham, which is on the A1067 just north west of Norwich. The pub stands on the edge of the village where the Taverham road meets two other small roads signposted to Costessey and Easton to the left and Ringland and Weston Longville to the right.

Parking: The pub has parking to the front and side or cars can be left near the pub on the public open space near the bridge.

Length of the walk: Just under 2 miles. OS Map Landranger series 133 North East Norfolk (GR 140138). There is a Broadland District Council leaflet describing a longer walk which incorporates part of this walk and adds a loop through woodland (see below). There is also an area of lovely wooded hills and heathland north west of the village (Ringland Hills) which is pleasant to explore.

The river Wensum describes a series of gentle curves on its way to Norwich and the pretty village of Ringland is caught in the midst of one of these loops. The walk leaves the area of the pub and the road bridge to climb a gentle hill out of the village which offers delightful views over the river valley to the wooded slopes on the other side of the river. It then follows a green lane round the edge of the river valley before

74

dropping down to walk alongside the watermeadows near a tributary of the main river.
When I walked there had been a lot of rain and the watermeadows were flooded,
offering a pleasant habitat for hundreds of waterfowl including a mass of swans. In
summer the route is good for wildflowers including pink and white campion and
yellow lesser celandine. Ringland is on the 'Tudor Tour' – a circular car route of
about 60 miles through historic towns and villages (leaflet available).

The Walk

Outside the pub is a signpost at a junction of small roads, showing
Costessey and Easton to the south, Ringland and Weston Longville to
the north and Taverham and Drayton to the east. Turn left and walk
in the direction of Ringland and Weston Longville. Pass Swan Cottage
on the left and other village dwellings. Soon on the right is a green
with the Ringland village sign, beautifully carved in wood in 1977,
with villagers' signatures on the support post set in the middle. Ahead
there are some interesting cottages with crow stepped gables, a feature
of the village.

Turn right at the green and follow a broad track past brick Pitt
Cottages, converted from barns, on the right to a junction of lanes
with the driveway to the Old Vicarage straight ahead.

There are two signposted (and arrow marked) paths to the left of the
Old Vicarage driveway. The furthest to the left can be taken to make
a longer walk bearing right and right again to join the route of this
walk.

For this shorter walk, however, take the broad right hand track and
go uphill along the edge of a field on the left with the driveway to the
Old Vicarage running alongside on the right. There is a really lovely
view over the extensive river Wensum valley and a background of
beautiful trees cladding the slope on the other side of the river. Note
the nice old cart standing to one side of the drive. Pass the Old
Vicarage on the right. The field on the left comes to an end at a
hedgerow which comes in from the left. Continue straight on into the
next field walking along a tree-studded hedgerow on the right with
another broad field on the left. At the end of the field there is a stile
with more footpath arrows. Cross this and take the footpath to the
right, crossing another stile to the left of a metal gate.

If preferred, you can instead go left here for the longer loop walk
mentioned above, which brings you back via a left turn to a road
where you turn left again to pass the church on the right and continue
on down through Ringland village back to the pub.

For the shorter walk, continue to the right along a broad grassy lane
with hedges on both sides. Pass a stand of old oak trees on the left.
Across the river on the left glimpses can be caught of a golf course.
At some time in the past this lane has been metalled and in places the

track emerges from the grass surfaced with flints. The hedge on the left ends but the broad grassy track continues on along the edge of watermeadows and a tributary of the river Wensum on the left. Pass a small copse on the left and then a cluster of farm buildings and a cottage with green shutters in an idyllic situation.

Continue on along the track which now becomes more stony and rutted. The riverside scenery is wooded and interspersed with occasional stands of poplar trees. Pass some sheds. There is now a good view of Ringland church ahead standing high on a slope above the village with a clustered huddle of roofs below. 13th century St Peter's has a magnificent hammer-beamed and vaulted roof and much excellent 15th century stained glass in the clerestory windows as well as a lovely painted screen base.

The stony track veers off to the left. Carry on along a more grassy track towards the houses of Ringland ahead. The conifer studded drive to the Old Rectory is now on the brow of the hill on the right. Pass a converted red brick barn on the left. Bear left down the track back to the green again and then left down the road back to the pub.

18 Burgh St Peter (Wheatacre)
The White Lion

In the late 18th century, a wherryman who operated out of Lowestoft built his house on a piece of high land so that he could see his boats go by on the river Waveney. The building, with its simple, restrained appearance under a mellow pantiled roof, eventually became the White Lion pub. It stands on its own in a pleasant garden surrounded by trees, fields and orchards, and is set back from a lane leading from Burgh St Peter to Wheatacre just near the boundary of the neighbouring parish of Aldeby, an old Viking settlement.

The White Lion is a useful place to take the family for a drink with tables outside to sit out in pleasant surroundings in summer. Good dogs are welcome in the pub. The bar is one big room with a woodburning stove at one end giving out comforting warmth in winter, while at the other end is a dartboard and pool table.

Take a picnic lunch with you as no food is available. However, you are welcome to eat your own food inside the pub provided that you have a drink from the bar. The pub is a freehouse which keeps to usual opening hours and there is a good range of beers on offer. The choice is between Adnams Bitter, Worthington's, M & B Mild and

Carling lagers. Strongbow cider and Murphy's Stout are also on draught and there is a selection of lagers.

Telephone: (Aldeby) 01502 677388.

How to get there: Burgh St Peter can be reached by turning off the A143 Yarmouth to Bungay road immediately south of the village of Haddiscoe. Follow the signs along a series of small lanes. The pub is south of Wheatacre church on the lane leading to Burgh St Peter.

This area is cut off by the river Yare so to avoid taking lengthy detours along main roads the approach from the north into this isolated section of Norfolk is via the small four car ferry at Reedham – an interesting experience.

Parking: There is a large car park to the front of the pub or alternative parking at Burgh St Peter staithe, halfway round the walk.

Length of the walk: 5 miles. OS Map Landranger series 134 Norwich and the Broads (GR 464936).

This is a curious finger of south Norfolk which has almost the feeling of an island. It lies within a loop of the river Waveney as it curls round to meet the sea at Great Yarmouth. On the other side of the river is Suffolk with Lowestoft to the east. The countryside round Burgh St Peter is fascinating. The spine of the finger of land is quite high and is home to mixed farming and small scattered settlements with isolated churches. There are many farmhouses sprinkled along the marsh edge. The land drops quite sharply to the low level of the marshes and there are lovely extensive views over these and the river valley in a northerly, easterly and southerly direction towards Yarmouth, Lowestoft and Beccles. The walk takes field paths just above the marsh edge to reach the staithe where there is a well-camouflaged marina and caravan park, just below the atmospheric church of St Mary's, stuck out like a beacon in the marsh. It then follows undulating lanes with marsh and river views back to Burgh St Peter.

The Walk

Turn left out of the pub which is on a side road and turn left again at a road junction down Beccles Road, signposted to Burgh St Peter. Pass the Wheatacre and Burgh St Peter village sign on the left and an abandoned school of 1877 on the right. Just past the post office and shop and houses on the left, turn left down Pit Road at a crossroads passing scattered dwellings. Walk past Crimp Cramp Lane which comes in on the left and then past Church Lane which comes in opposite a willow hung pond on the right. Pit Road changes into Oaks Lane which passes orchards on the left.

At a T junction, cross the main road (Burgh Road) and continue ahead down a broad track on the other side. Over the field ahead and

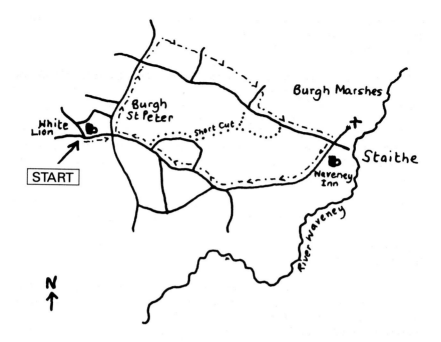

slightly to the left there is a view of the white swing bridge at Somerleyton a couple of miles away. This sunken green lane has probably been used for centuries as a drove road for stock being taken to and from the marshes.

Just before a belt of trees, turn right along a broad sandy track skirting along the edge of woodland. Bear right at a junction of tracks up towards a field. Turn left along the edge of the field (the right of way is marked at intervals by plastic arrows on posts) along the edge of the woodland which slopes down to the marsh on the left. A hedgerow comes down on the right near farm buildings on the left. Go through this and carry on ahead onto a farm track. Walk past the farmhouse on the left. Go through the wooden posts of a gateway and carry on ahead towards the next farm through the middle of a field, hopefully the path will be delineated. The route actually runs more or less from one farmhouse to the next through the fields. Come onto a stony track which leads to Carr Farm buildings and continue ahead on this. Then continue ahead across another field with tractor tracks showing the way. The roofs of a farm appear fairly well to the left ahead. There is also a view of the curious tower of Burgh St Peter church on the edge of the marsh in the distance. The track through

79

the field goes straight towards a gaunt dead tree and there is a rough wooden footpath sign by the edge of the farm track here. The official path should continue on and pass through the grounds of Holly Farm but it is easier to turn right up the track here to the road.

For a short cut back to the pub turn right for a short way here then left across an arable field following the finger of a footpath signpost to reach a road. Turn right here and bear right at the next juction, then right again along a more main road, staying on this through the village of Burgh St Peter to reach the pub.

For the main walk, turn left down the road and continue on past red brick Hall Farm on the left to a road junction. Turn right here for a second chance to join the short cut. Otherwise, continue on along Burgh Road passing cottages overlooking the marsh on the left. At the end of the lane is the Waveney Inn (closed from November to April) and Waveney River Centre for camping, caravanning and boating. A ferry used to operate from here to enable people to take a short cut to Oulton Broad and Lowestoft.

Take the lane on the left, signposted to the church and Goose Cottage only, for a detour to take a closer look at the interesting church. The unusual red brick pyramidal tower cut off at the top is 18th century on a 16th century base and is a landmark for boats right on the edge of the marshes by the river. The rest of the church is of knapped flint under a long thatched roof.

For the return journey follow the road round, passing the entrance drive to the Waveney Inn and its splendid sign depicting a Norfolk wherry on the left. This is Staithe Road and the signpost points ahead to Burgh St Peter (1 ½ miles). The road rises quite sharply and there is a steep drop on the left where caravans shelter beneath the lee of the cliff. The road goes gently downhill with arable fields on the right and the marshes, criss-crossed with dikes and waterways, are way down on the left. There are lovely views towards Suffolk. The nearer countryside is undulating and patchworked with woods and copses. The route of the walk is easy to follow now as you simply stick to the main road passing a few cottages and houses (one on the right is The Old Rectory) going straight on towards Burgh St Peter.

Carry on past a turning to the left. Avoid another turn to the left, then further on pass a broad track to the right. The lane curves and rises and falls gently making for the houses of Burgh St Peter – a somewhat straggling settlement. Pass a turn on the right where the short cut joins. Pass the Methodist chapel of 1864 which is now the village hall. At a crossroads Mill Lane goes to the left leading past houses to the stump of an old mill. The right hand turn is Pit Road where the walk set out. Continue straight on, retracing your footsteps past the shop and back to the pub.

Halvergate
The Red Lion

The pub sign is rather splendid – a rampant red lion with extremely ferocious-looking blue claws. Outside the pub is a long, low cream building with an old thatched roof. Inside the atmosphere of the open bars is warm and friendly, with a woodburning stove at one end of the bar. The low beamed ceiling is decorated with horse brasses and the walls are hung with interesting old photos of Halvergate. The Red Lion, which is on the Weavers' Way, is an unpretentious village pub with a traditional character, and is used by the locals as a place to drop into for a friendly pint.

The pub offers a selection of Carlsberg Tetley beers, lagers and ciders as well as Guinness and regularly changed guest ales including local brews. The menu is mainly sandwiches and snacks and is served at lunchtimes only from Easter through the summer. Bring your own sandwiches during winter months. The pub is closed Monday lunchtime. There are tables outside at the front, and dogs are welcome outside.

Telephone: (Great Yarmouth) 01493 700317.

81

How to get there: Halvergate is reached by turning off the B1140 road from Acle to Reedham or there is a turning off the A47 Norwich to Great Yarmouth road soon after Acle.

Parking: The pub has its own car park or there is space in the village.

Length of the walk: 5 miles. OS Map Landranger series 134 Norwich and the Broads (GR 423070).

This is a wonderful walk for a good clear day when you can see for miles over the marshes with a beneficial sense of space all around. The area of Halvergate Marshes is very special. It is one of the last remaining stretches of unimproved grazing marsh in Norfolk and is designated an Environmentally Sensitive Area where there is a scheme to pay farmers not to plough and to continue traditional grazing practices. The walk begins in an almost cosy way along lanes leading to the hamlet of Wickhampton where hedges and copses soften the landscape. Once past the church, however, the route leads directly into the marshes which stretch out in what seems like unbroken infinity towards Great Yarmouth. The only punctuation marks are the occasional farm or marshman's cottage, one or two lonely trees and of course the windmills which rise up from the marshes in various states of repair, from stumps only up to the full glory of cap and sails. The path leads along so-called 'walls' – raised banks in a waterlogged landscape, usually edged with ditches and dikes and crossed every now and again by plank bridges known as 'liggers'. Even so in wet weather these walls can become very muddy and are churned up by the feet of the cattle moved from area to area on the marsh for grazing in the spring, summer and autumn months. This walk meets up with the Weavers' Way which it follows across the marsh and onto a hard lane leading back into the village of Halvergate. A splendid area for all kinds of birds, though short-eared owls are a speciality.

The Walk

Turn right out of the pub. Pass a side road – Chapel Road which leads to a rather incongruous-looking yellow brick Methodist chapel of 1878 standing in splendid isolation in a field.

Turn left down a lane leading to Wickhampton Road passing through housing of varying ages. If you wish to visit Halvergate's St Peter and St Paul's church with its 16th century brass, take a detour right up here. Otherwise, pass a lane on the left called rather optimistically The City. There is a lovely view over the marshes on the left – on a clear day you can see Yarmouth. Pass an old farmyard on the right and continue along this pretty lane with overgrown hedging and the imposing Halvergate Hall and then the cricket and recreation ground on the right. Beyond is Halvergate windmill. Mutton's Mill is over the marsh on the left. Wickhampton church stands out ahead.

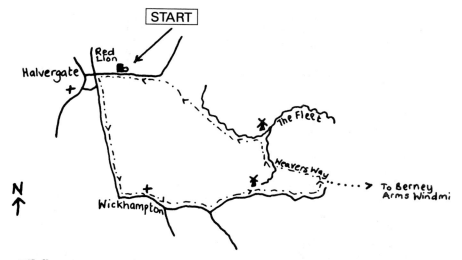

The lane continues through farming land where the trees over on the left housed a heronry until a few years ago.

At a T junction turn left into Wickhampton. Pass cottages and The Old Rectory on the right and continue straight ahead at a road junction down Church Road signposted 'To The Marshes Only'. Pass pleasant old thatched cottages and a red brick barn to arrive at the church. St Andrew's, with its beautiful knapped flint tower and porch, should be visited. It has some interesting wall paintings, some very early tombs with splendid effigies, and a fine 17th century pulpit. Take the broad stony track to the right of the church and before long go through a gateway onto a concrete farm track leading to the marshes and pass a metal cattle pound. The marsh on the left is often flooded in winter and attracts many swans. The view includes two windmills and a marshman's cottage in a clump of trees. Kerry's Mill, standing black amongst the trees, and Mutton's Mill are named after the marshmen who used to operate them and were involved with all the complexities of marsh drainage.

Avoid a track to the right and continue on along the concrete track with a broad ditch on the left. There is a public footpath signpost almost falling into the ditch on the right. Over on the right is a pleasant copse of mixed trees. The track is now in the middle of the marshes and everywhere you look are windmills in various states of repair. In the distance ahead can be seen Berney Arms Mill which is completely restored and stands on Breydon Water where the river Yare broadens out before it reaches Great Yarmouth. On a clear day, you can look out to the right over the Yare and Waveney rivers and see Suffolk.

Where the track comes to a T junction, turn left and go through a metal gate onto a grassy track. This is the Wickhampton Wall on the marsh proper with deep ditches on both sides. Mutton's Mill is now close to the path on the left hand side with the marshman's cottage beyond. Follow the track round past a cattle pound on the right passing various gates on the left and continue on. The occasional small train trundles through the marshes on the right travelling from Reedham to Great Yarmouth and making occasional stops at Berney Arms Halt. The track swings to the left quite sharply and winds round. Negotiate a metal gate and follow the track as it bends sharply to the left near more compounds for cattle, heading towards two isolated hawthorn trees. It arrives at a fenced area at a junction of tracks marked with Weavers' Way signs. The path to the right carries on to the Berney Arms windmill and pub which could make a pleasant detour.

For the main walk, follow the signpost to the left, cross a stile and walk through the middle of a marshy field towards a bridge and the marshman's cottage hidden in trees beyond. Bulls run with the herds which graze on the marshes in summer but are no danger. Cross a gated wooden bridge and continue ahead in the same direction making for a gateway to the right of the cottage. Cross the stile to the left of a metal gate and continue along the wall to the right in the direction of Mutton's Mill.

Then take a left turn over a stile and over a bridge crossing the Fleet Dike. Cross another stile by a wooden gate and follow the Weavers' Way to the right towards Mutton's Mill. The path swings to the left. Bear right over a stile to the left of a metal gateway leading over a concrete bridge. A spur of the Weavers' Way here going to the right leads all the way to Yarmouth.

This walk turns left (following the Weavers' Way in the other direction) along a high wall with one arm of the Fleet Dike on the left. The track winds gently through the marshes. Cross a stile to the right of a metal gate and continue on along the bank which curves to the right towards another cattle pound. Cross the stile to the left of this and cross a second stile to meet a metalled roadway. Turn left down this in the direction of Halvergate village. At a junction with the main road turn left and follow the road into the village, passing housing on the right back to the Red Lion pub.

20 **Bramerton**
The Woods End

Tiny bendy lanes lead to this riverside pub in the Woods End area of Bramerton not far east of Norwich. It stands in an idyllic situation near a wide bend of the river Yare overlooking watermeadows on the other side of the river and has a grassy garden overhung with a tree clad slope behind. More trees mass on the horizon, and huge flocks of water birds crowd the water and the meadows. Picnic tables are set out by the riverside to make the most of the scenery. The pub has quite a history. The front part of the building dates from 1885 but the rest is older. Originally an inn to service the wherries plying up and down the river (complete with George and Albert, the ghosts of two wherrymen), it was leased as an inn and tearoom in Victorian times, providing a pleasure ground for hundreds of trippers who arrived by the steamers *Doris* and *Jenny Lind* from Norwich. Billy, a local man, would race the steamers back to Norwich.

The Woods End is open from 11 am-11 pm from Easter but its winter hours can be erratic (worth a phone call to check). Food is served from 12 noon-2.30 pm and from 7 pm-9 pm. Cream teas from 3 pm-6.30 pm. The homemade steak and ale pie is good and so is the fresh fish which changes depending on what is available.

It was wing of skate and chargrilled sardines when I called. The specialities change every day. Various steaks can be ordered, and on Sundays there is a roast. The pub is a freehouse and rings the changes with real ales varying between Adnams Bitter and changing guest ales (a wider choice in summer). Scrumpy Jack cider is on draught. Children are welcome in the restaurant which opens onto the children's play area in the garden.

Telephone: (Surlingham) 01508 538899.

How to get there: Take the A146 out of Norwich in the direction of Loddon and Lowestoft. Not long after the A47 ring road go left onto a minor road signposted to Bramerton, turning left to Kirby Bedon and following the lane on to Woods End and the river and pub.

Parking: There is plenty of parking to the front and side of the pub or at nearby Bramerton Common.

Length of the walk: 5 miles. Go well shod and trousered, as you may encounter some muddy and overgrown paths. OS Map Landranger series 134 Norwich and the Broads (GR 290062).

It is well worth doing the whole of this figure of eight walk as it passes through very varied countryside encompassing woods, fields, gorgeous river scenery and an RSPB nature reserve, haunt of the little grebe, the marsh harrier and various kinds of warbler. However there are various opportunities for short cuts. Alternatively, the walk can be done in two separate circular sections, one starting from the Woods End Tavern and the other from the Ferry House pub further along the river.

The Walk

Turn left out of the pub and walk for a short distance up the tiny wooded approach lane. As it bends sharply to the right, turn left through a gateway and go up a wide grassy track (bridleway signpost). There are woods on the left and a field on the right. The track passes along the nice old wall of Bramerton House doing a little dog leg round the end of the wall and then carrying straight on. It eventually goes uphill passing houses on the left to reach a lane. Turn left and carry on, passing a turn to the left. The lane becomes a tunnel through overhanging trees. Pass Bramerton village hall and bowls club on the left and the grounds of Bramerton Hall on the right.

Turn left for a short distance at the main road, then left again down Mill Hill where there is a signpost to the pub. For a short cut follow this lane back to the pub. For the main walk turn right into Hill House

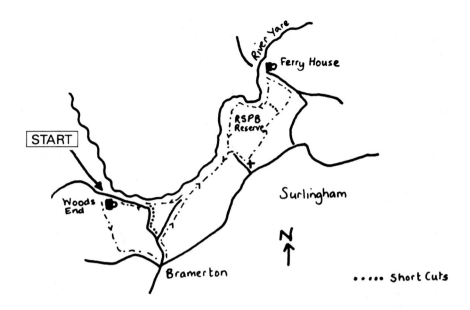

Road (no through road). Over the hedge on the left is a view down into the river valley and then the outskirts of Norwich beyond. Pass a scattering of houses to reach bargeboarded Hill House. Go ahead down a rutted track (Private Road) which leads to the river. For another short cut turn left behind a riverside cottage and follow the path along the river and back to the pub. To continue the main walk, turn right by the edge of the river through a white gate in a garden fence (a notice says 'Private. Public Footpath. Please Close Gate'), and continue on along a path edging a garden on the right and out of the gate on the other side. Bear right along a diverted permissive path uphill, then left at a footpath signpost along a narrow path through woods. The path then runs alongside a wood on the right with reed marsh and the river on the left. Carry on along this somewhat overgrown path ignoring a small bridge leading left to the river.

Near a thatched house, the path turns right to go uphill alongside a garden, then left between wire fencing to reach a lane. Turn right uphill and follow the lane round to St Mary's church at Surlingham, with its Norman round tower. Turn left, ignoring the wide path ahead, next to a flint cottage signposted to an RSPB reserve. Then almost immediately turn right following the church wall on the right down a broad lane passing a couple of houses. Soon a large RSPB board on the left gives details of the Surlingham Church Marsh Reserve. It was formerly used for summer grazing of cattle and the cutting of sedge and hay. Eventually, it became neglected, the dikes ceased to function and the river water polluted the area. Under RSPB management the river water has been excluded and the dikes cleared out and maintained to restore the diversity of wildlife. It is especially good for wild flowers. The famous local naturalist, Ted Ellis, is buried here and nearby Wheatfen Broad is a memorial to him.

Climb the stile near the board or go through the gateway onto the reserve (footpath signpost) and continue down a broad grassy track shortly turning right to follow it on alongside a fenced off meadow on the right and the marsh on the left. There is a small cottage complex on the right where a shooting club operates from time to time so stick to the public path which is quite narrow and overgrown. Continue on, passing a steep meadow to the right. A stile on the left takes a public footpath onto the reserve to reach the river bank. This again can be used for a short cut turning left along the river bank and following the route of the walk back to the pub.

The main walk continues on along the path ahead crossing a stile to the right into the meadow and then following the hedge to the left towards houses. Cross two stiles near a barn on the right to reach a lane. Turn left down the lane through trees to the Ferry House pub by the river. There was once a ferry crossing here, one of several ferries crossing the river Yare. Turn left along the river bank and cross a stile leading onto a permissive path marked with a dragonfly. Carry on for a mile or so along this narrow path edging the river, crossing a wooden footbridge over a dike to reach the RSPB reserve where the short cut footpath mentioned earlier joins the riverbank path. After passing near two hides, the track leaves the main river and goes alongside a watery cut on the right. Pass another Reserve notice on the left and continue uphill through encroaching hedges going through a gateway near the flint cottage on the left (mentioned earlier) to reach Surlingham church again.

From here follow the outward route back again taking the lane to the right to reach the thatched house. Turn left then right downhill alongside the garden towards the river, then turn left again to follow the path through woods with the marshes and river on the right. Negotiate the white garden gates by the river again. Do not go up the rutted lane to Hill House, but go through a white gate behind a single storey cottage and follow a narrow path through another white gate onto a wide grassy bank where there are boat moorings. This is part of Bramerton Common. Go ahead passing a parking area at the bottom of Mill Lane onto a little roadway at Woods End, passing modern houses on the left to return to the pub.

㉑ Ranworth
The Maltsters Inn

This Scottish and Newcastle pub, which was a coaching inn dating from 1762, stands in a lovely position overlooking Malthouse Broad and staithe. The interior looks very modern and has been designed on a nautical theme with portholes and ships' accessories. An unusual feature inside is a section of a boat – the *M Y Ranworth* built by H.T. Percival Boat Builders of Horning in 1948 – which protrudes into one end of the restaurant to make a family room with a pool table (which stands outside in summer) and a pinball machine and opens onto the garden. The restaurant is clean, airy and pleasant with modern furniture and a piano. The bar area is decorated with photos of old Broadland scenes and there are fishing rods on the wall. A talking point is the animal in the glass case – is it a young otter, a large stoat or a polecat? No one seems to know.

The Maltsters, probably named after the workmen from the Old Maltings who frequented it, is open all day in summer from July to September and serves food every day. It has a board on which specialities are written and a Sunday lunch of roast beef is cooked all year round. The menu is small and simple but reasonably priced. Vegetarians are catered for and there is a special children's menu.

Beers include Woodforde's and Directors and various guest beers throughout the year. Strongbow cider is on tap. There are picnic tables on hard standing at the front to take advantage of the view and a small grassy area of garden. Dogs are not allowed inside the pub but will no doubt be happy to wait in this lovely area.
Telephone: (South Walsham) 01603 270241.

How to get there: Ranworth is 1 mile north of South Walsham down a small lane off the B1140 which runs between Acle and Norwich. The road leads directly to the pub.

Parking: Opposite the pub with useful public lavatories at one side, or at the Ranworth Broad Conservation Centre car park.

Length of the walk: Less than 4 miles of gently undulating walking. OS Map Landranger series 134 Norwich and the Broads (GR 360146).

Typical Broadland scenery is the hallmark of this enchanting walk most of which is along tiny quiet lanes. The Broads originated as peat diggings excavated between the 9th and the 14th centuries. The pits were between 5 ft and 15 ft deep and gradually as the level of the sea rose over the centuries, they became flooded and were abandoned. Cuts were dug to aid access to villages and the waterways were used for freight. Ranworth and Malthouse Broads attracted a great mass of wildfowl and plenty of shooting took place until the 1940s. From the route, there are lovely views of three different broads and the surrounding marshes framed in swathes of lovely trees of varying ages which offer some shelter from wind. The walk is dominated in each direction by different views of Ranworth church which stands high on a spur of land on the outskirts of the village. Its tower is open to the public and offers splendid views over Broadland. The walk passes Ranworth Broad Nature Reserve where a fascinating nature trail, showing different sections of the marsh from a boardwalk, leads to the unusual floating timber and thatch Broadland Conservation Centre. This has informative displays on the history and wildlife of the Broads and explains the pressures threatening Broadland today. Upstairs the gallery has a superb view over the broad.

The Walk

Leave the pub and bear left to the road junction, turning right along a lane signposted to the marshes passing the staithe where malt used to be brought by great wherries for malting locally, and the Granary Stores which is attached to a lovely thatched cottage. A little further on is a parking area for the Ranworth Broad Conservation Centre on the right. The lane goes past various scattered houses and cottages and ends at Leists Farm becoming a broad sandy track. Go ahead along this pretty track with views over Ranworth Marshes on the left.

At a fork bear sharply to the right and continue to follow the track. The views are more open here and the path is lined with ancient oaks. The track bears left and goes downhill. Follow the narrow path along the edge of a copse beyond which can be seen glimpses of South Walsham Broad. Eventually, at a fork, bear right up a gravelly lane near houses and cottages. Cross over a road and walk down the lane opposite passing a couple of houses and then out into the countryside. The lane wanders for over a mile through hedges beyond which lovely woods surround the fields. There are good views of Ranworth church standing high on its spur through gaps on the right. Follow the road downhill round bends near a copse. At a crossroads turn right and follow the bends of another small lane for about ¾ mile passing orchards on the left.

The lane arrives at a crossroads opposite St Helen's church. There is a panoramic view from the tower over Ranworth and Malthouse Broads, and over to the river Bure and the ruins of St Benet's Abbey. Near Ranworth Broad can be seen the early 17th century Old Hall. The church is mainly 14th century and has a wonderful painted rood screen of 1470 said to be the best in England. Also on display is a lovely illuminated manuscript of about 1400, the 'Sarum Antiphoner' created by monks from Langley a few miles away over the marshes. The roof was of thatch until an unfortunate fire in 1963. Cross and walk down the lane opposite which runs between high banks, passing timber and thatch Ranworth village hall on the right.

Bear sharply to the right here. On the left is the access path to the nature trail, Conservation Centre and shop on Ranworth Broad run by the Norfolk Wildlife Trust. It is well worth the short detour to look at this. The trail passes through oak woodland, wet woodland, called swamp carr, and open fen to the edge of the broad. Birds include nuthatches, spotted woodpecker, wren, treecreepers, reed warblers, fieldfares and waxwings as well as a mass of water birds on the broad — and this is a tiny sample of the great quantity of species to be seen here. Alder and sallow trees colonise the carr, and silver birch and ash indicate higher ground. There are areas of lichen and mosses as well as royal ferns, primroses, wild hop, water lilies, guelder rose, milk parsley, purple loosestrife, and orange balsam providing food for insects and butterflies, among them the rare swallowtail. The reed is grown commercially for thatching.

On leaving the reserve continue along the lane passing various houses with good views over Malthouse Broad. At the main road turn left to reach the pub again.

22 Horsey
The Nelson Head

This small cottagey pub is set in an isolated position on the edge of marshy fields leading up to the high dunes which hold back the sea. There is an area of grass with benches at the side for sitting out in good weather, and a 36 seater marquee which is used as a dining room providing protection from the elements. Inside, as befits the pub name, the theme is nautical. There are plaques of Lord Nelson and Lady Hamilton on either side of the fireplace and the bar which is divided into two areas, is decorated with ships' lamps, a steering wheel, rope, an anchor, a porthole mirror, a boathook and even a bilge pump. There is a dartboard at one end of the warmly carpeted bar and the furnishings are simple tables, some large benches and modern wheelback chairs. There is a separate small dining room where families can sit.

The pub is freehold and features delicious home-cooked food including fresh local fish and meat with vegetables from nearby farm shops. Puddings tend to be traditional such as apple pie, and vegetarians are well catered for. All food is homemade. A special 'twitcher's' lunch is available instead of the more usual ploughman's.

This is a choice of fresh cooked ham, cheddar cheese, pâté, or smoked mackerel with salads, pickle and a roll and butter. Meals are served every day within usual opening hours though summer hours may be a little longer. Real ales include Woodforde's Wherry, and Nelson's Revenge. Murphy's and Blackthorn Dry cider are on draught and a selection of lagers is available.

Telephone: (Winterton-on-Sea) 01493 393378.

How to get there: Horsey is 1 mile from the coast midway between Sea Palling and Winterton-on-Sea on the B1159 road. The pub is a short way down a left turn off this main road, in the centre of the village.

Parking: In the pub car park, in the National Trust car park near Horsey Mere, or by Horsey Gap.

Length of the walk: 5 miles of flat walking. A short cut is possible. OS Map Landranger series 134 Norwich and the Broads (GR 461229).

Choose a fine and not too windy day to do this walk as there is little shelter. You will be rewarded by a superb contrast between the wild seashore and huge protective dunes and tranquil grazing meadows, river and marsh. The walk passes along lanes leading to the beach which were used by smugglers in days gone by. The contraband was dumped from ships onto the beach and taken by horse and cart to Horsey where it was to be loaded onto wherries for distribution inland. The landscape is punctuated by the magnificent towers of Norfolk churches and windmills, many of which sadly are derelict, although the walk passes the beautifully restored Horsey Drainage Mill. It is an odd experience to see sails floating through the middle of fields as much of the water of the broads and cuts is hidden by trees and reeds. This is an excellent walk for bird watchers.

The Walk

Leave the pub by the front door and turn left along a little lane. Turn left again at a fork down another lane which leads through marshy meadows, cropped in summer by cattle, towards the dunes. Go through a gap by a metal gate and keep ahead along a wide grassy track between fences. Pass through some marshy areas and little copses which provide an excellent habitat for birds. Go through a reinforced gap in the dunes and onto the beach. If it is very windy or the tide is high there is a footpath to the left on the landward side of the dunes. A plaque in Horsey sea wall dated 1988 marks the completion of 14 kilometres of sea defences from Horsey to Winterton. This area has suffered devastating flooding following breaches of the sea defences

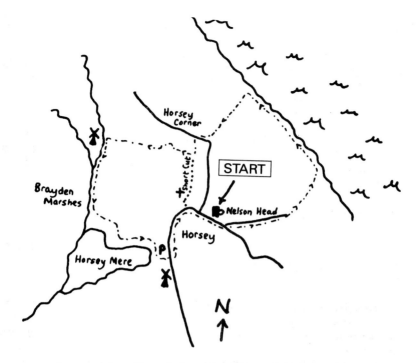

on several occasions. Turn left and walk along the wild and usually deserted beach for about a mile to reach another gap in the dunes (Horsey Gap).

Go through the dunes to the left and walk ahead through an area where cars can be parked, then down a track lined with bushy willows giving welcome shelter. The National Trust owns more than 2,000 acres at Horsey. The track continues onto a road at a bend. Turn right down the road for a short distance. Halfway along this short stretch which approaches houses, turn left down a track along a field edge with a ditch on the left and an open field on the right. For a short cut keep on ahead here following the track which eventually comes to a lane and Horsey church.

For the complete walk to the river and marshes, turn right at the first field boundary keeping the scrappy hedgerow on the right. Bear left then right round a garden, then go down a broad stretch to a lane (Horsey Corner). A signpost in the hedge here says that this is a Broads Authority Walk. Turn right down the lane for a very short distance then left at the next footpath signpost (dragonfly mark). Continue ahead down this narrow path passing a cottage on the left making for a derelict windmill. Cross a wooden footbridge and then a stile onto a bank, then bear left and then right along the bank towards the mill. There are wide views across the grazing meadows towards woods, and flocks of greylag geese rise into the skies. The remains of several windmills can be seen across the marshes and sails float past through the fields on the left. Cross another stile and keep on ahead to Brogrove windmill. Climb a third stile and go up onto the bank which borders the river (the New Cut).

Turn left along the bank for nearly a mile. The land is now part of the Horsey estate which is managed as a wildlife and conservation area and Brayden Marshes lie over the water on the right. Take care as this narrow path can be muddy and slippery at times. The path veers slightly to the left away from the water and skirts a reed bed. A notice asks walkers to follow a route marked with white discs. Go down wooden edge steps to the left onto a boardwalk, and bear right through reeds which hide Horsey Mere on the right. This 100 acre broad has slightly brackish water which has encouraged a rather special range of wildlife, differing from that in other broads. Cross a bridge over a ditch and then go over a stile into a meadow. Go straight ahead across the meadow to a white disc marker. Now sails can be seen on the mere and the low thatched roofs of boathouses edge the water. The path leads almost directly to Horsey Mill. Arriving at another white marker, cross a stile and a bridge and go up steps.

Walk to the left along the path between stunted willows and trees in the marsh on the left and the reeds edging Horsey Mere on the right. This pretty winding track offers lovely views over the mere. The track comes out at a cut providing good moorings for boats. Turn left and walk to the road at the end of the cut near Horsey Mill. This was built in the Victorian era to drain the surrounding land, but stopped working when it was struck by lightning in 1943. It has been restored by the National Trust and continues with its job of drainage albeit now with the help of an electric pump. There is a National Trust car park with toilets here, and a shop and snack hut nearer the mill (open in the summer season from the end of March until the end of August). Opposite the car park there is a track going across fields to the left to come out near the pub but this is only supposed to be used in the summer season. Instead turn left along the lane taking care as it can become quite busy especially in summer. Follow the bends of this tree-hung road to a junction at a corner. Turn left here to visit pretty Saxon thatched and octagonal-towered All Saints' church where the short cut footpath comes out. Otherwise turn right continuing along the main road passing scattered houses and cottages to a sharp left hand bend. Leave the main road here and carry on ahead along the minor road back to the pub.

23 **Buxton**
The Crown

The Crown is an interesting 18th century brick and cobble building graced with a decorative trefoil gable end. Inside, this freehouse is simple and unpretentious, serving well kept beers and a menu of bar snacks and sandwiches. Walking groups can be specially catered for if a phone call is made first. The usual real ale is Adnams Bitter, varied by different guest ales, often one from the Woodforde's stable. Guinness and Sam Smith's Yorkshire bitter are on draught as well as Strongbow cider. Tea and coffee are also available. The pub is open from 12 noon to 3 pm and from 6 pm to 11 pm Monday to Thursday. On Friday, Saturday and Sunday it is open all day (Sunday closing 10.30 pm). In the summer season the pub stays open all day every day.

There are two good sized bars, one of which has a pool table. The other bar has links with Douglas Bader who was stationed nearby. Tables are set up in the secluded garden outside in summer and children and dogs are welcome.

Telephone: 01603 279958.

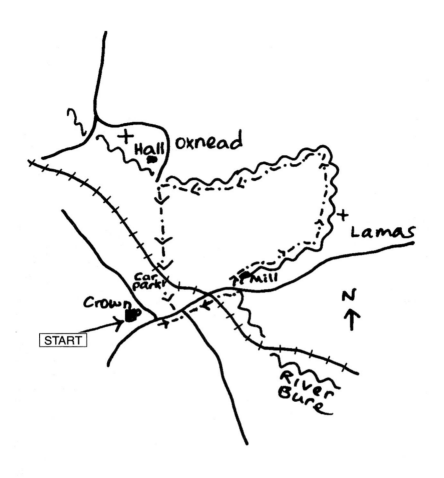

How to get there: Buxton is on the B1354 between Aylsham and Coltishall and the Crown is on the main road.

Parking: There is limited parking at the pub but there is a car park by the old railway line for the Bure Valley Walk and Railway (turn left after the Crown and before the church along Stracey Road, a housing estate).

Length of the walk: About 4½ miles of fairly flat walking. OS Map Landranger series 134 Norwich and the Broads (GR 238229).

The route from Buxton Mill along the river bank, passing a few houses of the village of Lamas on the opposite bank through woods and watermeadows to the ancient hall at Oxnead, gives the walker the impression of being wafted back in time to the days when the mill was in its prime, when the pace of life was more leisurely, and things were more simple. Oxnead itself is an enchanting hamlet with the remaining wing and garden terraces of Oxnead Hall by the river Bure, the lovely 13th century church and the romantic old mill which still stands nearby. It is not until you leave the enchanted area by the river and cut up through fields back towards Buxton and its former railway line that the spell is broken. Buxton itself must have been quite a lively place when the railway and mill were operational. Thomas Cubitt, the famous architect and builder of Victorian London, lived here at one time. A riverside walk also goes in the other direction to Wroxham.

The Walk

From the Crown follow the main road downhill to the church, which has lovely stained glass windows and a carved pulpit. Take the left fork, passing the mill stone which is Buxton's village sign and follow the road under a railway bridge bearing right round a corner to reach impressive Buxton Mill (a reconstruction of the original mill of 1754 which was destroyed by fire in 1991). Just before the Mill and river, leave the road and turn left between the Mill and a partially boarded large house. Follow the path through an alley leading to a modern house keeping close to the old buildings on the right, then bearing right to reach the river bank. Cross a stile and go left alongside the river on the right. Cross another stile at the end of a row of modern properties on the left and carry on along the river into open countryside. The scattering of houses and cottages and the church on the other side of the river make up the village of Lamas. Anna Sewell, author of *Black Beauty* is buried here in the Quaker Burial Ground. Cross another stile in a rickety fence and continue on along the raised river bank following the bends in the river. Cross a sort of bridge where another small waterway comes in and go through a metal gate (no sign of a stile).

Then cross a stile into a wood and continue on through a rather muddy section where the river sometimes floods over the path. There is a ditch on the left. The hamlet of Oxnead comes into view. The splendid remains of the terraced garden which surrounded 17th century Oxnead Hall, once the home of the famous Norfolk Paston family who entertained Charles II there in 1671, can be seen by the banks of the river. It is worth taking a detour to the right over the bridge to visit St Michael's church with its Paston monuments.

For the main walk, turn left at the bridge and walk down a broad track passing a small pumping building. Carry on to where the lane bends to the right. Go through by an iron gate off the main track and continue on uphill along a path through fields. Keep walking straight on at a crosstrack making for the houses of Buxton. Eventually the path meets the old railway track, now a narrow gauge line operated between Aylsham and Hoveton by the Bure Valley Railway Company. Alongside the line is the Bure Valley Walk and a leaflet about this is available from Broadland District Council. On the other side of the track is a gravelled car park and a notice explaining the walk. Cross the line carefully into the car park. To return to the Crown, bear left then immediately right, then left again through a housing estate (Stracey Road) and turn right along the main road back to the pub.

East Ruston
The Butcher's Arms

This simple but pleasant freehouse is set back off the road on the edge of the scattered village of East Ruston next to a large green. Picnic tables are set out in front to take advantage of the pleasant outlook over the green to the wooded alder carr across the road and there are more picnic tables in a patio area at the back. The two original bars have been knocked into one and there are three gaming machines to keep you busy. There are interesting old auction advertisements on the wall. The lounge end is warmed by an open fire in winter, with settles providing some of the seating. A collection of old lacrosse sticks and farming implements makes an unusual wall decoration. The lounge leads into a pretty restaurant at the side decorated in fresh blue tones.

The lunch and evening menus consist of a selection of wholesome and freshly cooked dishes (with no frozen ingredients). The fish comes straight off the quay at Lowestoft. There is always a choice of roasts at Sunday lunchtime and the reasonably priced menus are extended by special dishes which might include lamb shanks in rosemary and red wine sauce. Food is served from 12 noon-2 pm and from 7 pm-9 pm every day. The beers include Adnams Bitter, Bass,

Worthington, M & B Mild, with Caffreys as well as Guinness on draught. The real ales may change from time to time. Scrumpy Jack cider is also on draught. Dogs are welcome but not in the eating areas. The Butcher's Arms is the only pub I encountered which played classical music in the loos!

Telephone: (North Walsham) 01692 650237.

How to get there: Take the lane signposted to Honing off the A149 between North Walsham and Stalham. Continue on through Honing for a mile or so and the Butcher's Arms is on the right on the edge of the village of East Ruston.

Parking: Parking is available to the front and rear of the pub or next to the adjacent green. There is also a Weavers' Way car park near the dismantled railway line just on the outskirts of East Ruston.

Length of the walk: About 6 miles. OS Map Landranger series 134 Norwich and the Broads (GR 345282).

This walk explores part of the out of the way villages of East Ruston and Honing which have the great advantage of being surrounded by acres of beautiful common and fenland with a variety of wooded and reedy areas. It touches on the Weavers' Way (a 56 mile long distance route between Cromer and Great Yarmouth) which here goes along a disused railway line. The route of this walk heads off through fields to the banks of the Dilham Canal, originally the river Ant which was turned into a canal in 1826. Now disused except by small boats and fishermen, this enchanting waterway wanders through lovely countryside to reach the lock at Honing, now fallen into disrepair. It is a wonderful spot for wildlife of all kinds. The last part of the walk is along a twisting country lane leading from Honing to East Ruston bordered by more woods, fenland and commons.

The Walk

Turn right out of the pub and turn immediately right down the lane away from the more main road. After a short distance, turn into Youngman's Lane, a turning on the right, following its bends to right and left passing houses, then an area of common land on the right. At a crossroads, continue down the lane ahead signposted to Stalham. This is now Chapel Road. Pass the post office on the left and more houses with open fields and fenland on the right.

Bear left round the corner and very shortly bear right to the Weavers' Way which goes along the disused railway line here with a car park nearby. Do not go along the Way but cross it carrying on along a stony track ahead (public footpath signpost). Go through a gateway passing a flint crossing-keeper's cottage on the left with the

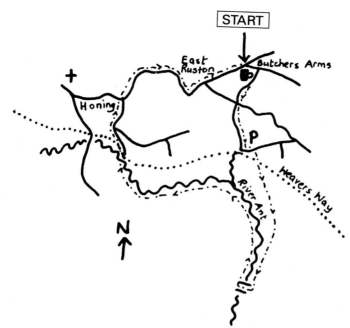

old white crossing gates on the field boundary opposite. Go through the gate ahead and continue on along the edge of a meadow by a barbed wire fence, ditch and hedgerow on the left. Cross a stile to the right of metal gates and continue on along a track (which can be very muddy) with a ditch on either side. Cross a stile to the right of a second metal gate, then cross the meadow here diagonally towards a pantiled roofed cottage over the field. Cross a stile next to a wooden gate and go along the edge of the Dilham Canal on the right towards a red brick bridge. Cross another stile just by the bridge.

Turn right over the bridge. A notice explains that Tonnage Bridge is part of the North Walsham-Dilham Canal system, built in the 1820s by widening the river Ant. It connects North Walsham with Great Yarmouth 25 miles away. It had 6 locks and 8 bridges. Shallow draught wherries came up here and their cargoes were weighed and tolls collected at the bridge. The sailing wherry, unique to Norfolk, was a huge clinker-built open boat with one long cargo hold covered with hatches. Today wherries can still be seen sailing in the Broads area with their huge gaffe-spread black sails. The canal was not too successful because it was too shallow to take most boats and commercial use stopped in the 1930s. The bridge was restored in 1982.

Carry on along the track leading to the bridge for a little way and before a white cottage turn off the track to the right down the towpath which is now just a small grassy track alongside the canal on the right. The track is lined with conifers for a short distance and then goes over a plank footbridge across a side stream. The route of the walk carries on alongside this lovely stretch of water for some distance and you may see large gatherings of swans. An arm of the river goes off in the direction of East Ruston on the right. Continue on passing another stretch of conifers and negotiating several plank bridges over dikes and ditches. A beautiful tree-studded area of fenland stretches out on the left. In a gap in a hedgerow go over a field bridge which crosses a wide side stream and continue on to a splendid gated and fenced wooden bridge over another broad stretch of water. Cross this, then go over a plank bridge to the right and cross a stile into woodland, carrying on over plank bridges through marshy woodland by the river to Honing Lock where the constricted river rushes through old lock walls.

Turn right over the footbridge over the lock. Follow the track over a plank footbridge through woodland to where the Weavers' Way crosses again. Go on over this and up a track past houses and cottages. Continue on up a roadway towards another knot of cottages. Honing church tower can just be seen beyond. At a junction of roads at a grassy triangle near cottages bear left and shortly after at the next junction turn right, signposted to East Ruston. The lane passes cottages on the left and part of Honing Common. At another junction of small roads continue on bearing left past houses to another junction. I avoided the footpath short cut on the OS map just here because it disappeared into heavy plough.

Turn right along the lane signposted to East Ruston. Follow the bends of this lane passing the occasional cottage. There is a lovely view of Honing church standing in its solitary position outside the village. Pass the junction leading to Crostwight Common. The road is bordered by beautiful tree strewn common and fen land and continues on over a white railinged bridge over a stream. Ignore a road to the right and carry on past houses to return to the Butcher's Arms on the right. The permissive footpath through the alder carr on the left of the road is worth exploring if you still have time and energy.

㉕ Blickling
The Buckinghamshire Arms

This three storied 17th century inn, which is owned by the National Trust, stands at an angle to the main road across a beautifully kept tree-studded green fronting onto a gravelly lane and the walled orchard of Blickling Hall. The building is part colourwashed and part mellow red brick with leaded window panes and a Dutch gable at one end. Behind on the lawn are tables under sunshades in summer backed by a sweep of gravel leading to a fine Dutch gabled barn.

The entrance is through double doors with a lantern outside and a small snug lies directly up a step ahead. This is dark and cosy, painted greenish blue, with lots of mellow wood brightened by a gleaming collection of old brass taps. To the left is the restaurant area which is really two rooms. The modern tables and windsor chairs are painted in a pleasing greyish-blue colour. Old bread ovens are set in the walls which are decorated with a large collection of Vanity Fair cartoons. There is a small hall with a display of local goodies. To the right of the snug is the lounge bar which has a woodburning stove in an old wooden fireplace. Everywhere the windows are softened by handsome curtains softly patterned in green.

The pub's day begins in summer with morning coffee, unless you are staying in one of the three bedrooms (all with four poster beds) when you will have been served a full English breakfast. At lunchtime the bar menu consists of various baguettes and snack meals as well as more elaborate fish, meat and vegetarian dishes. Special dishes of the day are written up on a blackboard with Betty's steak and kidney pie being a favourite. There is a good selection of puds including Betty's treacle tart. Bar meals are served every lunchtime and evening. Dinner is served from 7 pm to 9 pm every day. Sunday lunch is served from 12 noon with last orders at 2 pm. The dining room can be booked for parties of up to 40 people. Beers are local – from Adnams and Woodforde's with other guest beers. Strongbow cider is on draught. No dogs are allowed inside.

Telephone: (Aylsham) 01263 732133.

How to get there: Blickling is reached by the B1354, 1½ miles from Aylsham which is on the A140, north of Norwich. The pub is in the centre of the village next to the hall.

Parking: There is a car park behind the pub or a larger National Trust car park beyond the barn.

Length of the walk: 3½ miles mainly on tracks and lanes. OS Map Landranger series 133 North East Norfolk (GR 178286).

The walks round Blickling are well known but I could not resist including this one because the scenery is just glorious. The 17th century Blickling Hall with its pale red brick and creamy stone is the jewel in the National Trust's Norfolk crown. An earlier hall was Anne Boleyn's childhood home. It is surrounded by a beautiful park (designed in part by Humphrey Repton who is buried at nearby Aylsham) and farmland with parkland trees and woods which sweep down to the pretty valley of the river Bure. The walk goes through lovely undulating countryside with a patchwork of small fields and hedgerows, along the romantic tree-hung river Bure with its accompanying watermeadows, through large woods, small woods, and spinneys offering a wide variety of trees both ancient and newly planted. A mill and attractive estate cottages and barns punctuate the landscape. In the grounds of the Hall, the walk passes a lake which attracts a variety of waterfowl, and returns to the inn.

The Walk

Turn left out of the inn and walk along a lane bounded by the old red brick walls of the Hall grounds on the right. There are several very pretty estate cottages down this lane. At a junction of lanes near a tree encompassed by a wooden circular seat, bear right and continue on

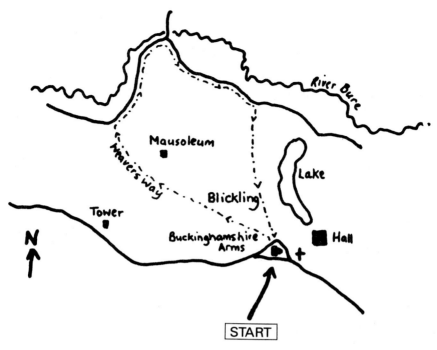

START

to a white park gate. Go through this and take the track to the left which is signposted Weavers' Way (a 56 mile walking route joining Cromer with Great Yarmouth). This is a wide stony track passing through fenced off fields at first with a view of the lake over the fields on the right. The fields are mature parkland dotted with lovely old trees with cattle cropping the grass beneath. The path continues on alongside woods on the right where dells mark old pits.

Go through a wooden gate and continue on through knots of woodland breaking up the more open parkland. The track arrives at a large section of woodland on the right where a board explains the woodland restoration policy of judicious felling and replanting. Continue on downhill through trees and then the Great Wood on the right. A track just before the Great Wood branches off to the right to reach the mausoleum – a stone pyramid built in about 1794 to mark the graves of John Hobart, Earl of Buckinghamshire and his two wives. At the bottom of the hill just before a wooden gate look left back to the red tower standing high between two hillocks. It was built in about 1773 as a viewpoint for races on a course which has now disappeared. Pass to the right of the wooden gate and carry straight on. Go through an open gateway onto a lane at a bend.

Turn right still following the Weavers' Way sign and passing a red brick cottage on the left. Go uphill alongside the Great Wood on the right with more woodland over the hill on the left. The lane passes a complex of barns on the left and a house on the right, and then bends to the right near the old mill cottage. The river Bure comes rushing under the arches of an old bridge and runs alongside the road on the left. Pass a pantiled cartshed on the left and a grove of poplar trees. There are some lovely riverside picnic spots along here. The Weavers' Way is signposted off to the left alongside the river and through the woods. This walk continues along the lane which bears quite sharply to the right and passes a small wooden barn on the right to come to the hamlet of Moorgate – a handful of cottages and small farmhouses.

As the cottages end turn right up a track with a wooden public footpath signpost and then continue on alongside the hedge on the right on a narrow path. Follow the tree-studded hedge as it curves to the right then the left. When the hedge ends continue straight on along a grassy baulk punctuated with ancient oaks – the division between two fields. At a crosstrack near a copse keep straight ahead along a broad track towards wooden gates with a stile to the left and a small gate to the right. Go ahead down a broad stony track with the lake over on the left and glimpses of the Hall itself at the end. Make for the white park gates passed near the beginning of the walk. Go through them and return down the lane to the inn.

It is worth doing a small extension to the walk and bearing left just beyond the pub, crossing the grass in front of the lovely wrought iron gates through which can be seen the south front of Blickling Hall framed by billowing yew hedges. To one side is a plant centre in a former walled orchard. There is a shop and a restaurant at the Hall. For opening hours telephone 01263 733084. The park is open daily. Continue on to explore the parish church of St Andrew which contains many monuments to people connected with the Hall including members of the Boleyn family. To reach it, go up steps from the main gate and then out at the gate on the other side. Turn right, cross the road and go a little way down Silvergate – the lane on the other side. A stile to the right leads to an interesting ice house.

26 **Happisburgh**
The Hill House

The Hill House is in a splendid position set right on the clifftop up an alleyway next to the church. It is a listed building originally built in the 16th century, but renovated in 1710. It has been an inn since coaching days as the large gates leading to stables behind indicate. The stables are now converted into a function room which seats 40 and becomes a popular family room in the holiday season as it opens onto the garden where food is served in summer and there is a barbecue. Coaching routes were often followed by the railways and there was a plan to bring the Great Eastern line along a branch to Happisburgh. The supporting services including a clinker-wood signal box at the back of the pub were built but in the end the plan was abandoned. However, the signal box, now rendered, remains as a family bed and breakfast room (more B & B rooms in pub) with a sea view from huge windows at first floor level. The main part of the pub has a through bar with a pool table and darts at one end, leading to a lounge area with curved velvet banquette seats and velvet topped stools. This has a big inglenook fireplace where fires are lit in winter. The wealth of old timber in the bars is said to have come from wrecked ships. There is a restaurant leading off the lounge.

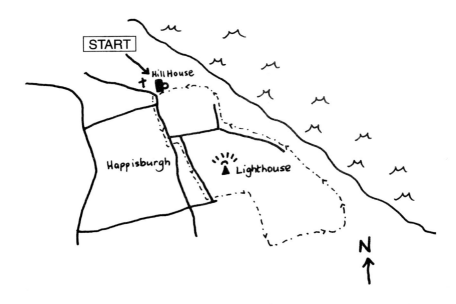

The restaurant menu is quite extensive with some interesting starters such as chicken tikka and Stilton egg. There are standard main courses with different specialities every few days and the seasonal weekend special is a large fresh seafood platter. The bar snack menu offers a variety of sandwiches (plain and toasted) as well as six kinds of ploughman's and eight kinds of jacket potatoes. In addition, there is a hot weekday lunch for £2, together with the usual grills and burgers and a children's and vegetarian menu. Usual opening hours apply though the pub stays open all day in the summer season and from Thursday to Sunday inclusive for the rest of the year. Bussy's Elementary beer is special to the Hill House and usually five other real ales are on offer. The draught cider is Stowford Press. The restaurant is no smoking throughout, and dogs are allowed in the pub on leads.

The Hill House is regularly visited by the Sherlock Holmes Society as Conan Doyle wrote some of his stories here including *The Dancing Men*. One can imagine that the atmosphere on this wind-swept cliff on a dark, stormy night could be most scary!

Telephone: (Walcott) 01692 650004.

How to get there: Happisburgh is on the north east Norfolk coast on the B1159 road between Bacton and Sea Palling. Hill House is in the centre of the village.

Parking: There is a car park in front of the pub or a pay and display car park on the clifftop near the coastguard station.

Length of the walk: 2 miles of easy walking. OS Map Landranger series 133 North East Norfolk (GR 380311).

Exhilarating views over wind-torn fields to prominent church towers, or out over a foaming sea with waves crashing against the bottom of the cliffs, make this an exciting walk even in the relative tranquillity of a summer's day. The walk links the history of this pretty village and its splendid church with its beacon tower and graveyard of sailors to the dangerous sea at its feet watched over by the brooding red and white striped lighthouse built in 1791. The sea reaches right under the cliff here so don't be tempted to walk far along the beach if the tide is coming in.

The Walk

Leave the pub and walk down the small lane leading to it. Bear left at the main road passing the Happisburgh village sign situated behind a garden wall (this painted sign shows a christening at the 15th century carved font, the church and the lighthouse). Continue along the pavement on the right hand side passing the attractive Happisburgh school built of decorative bricks in 1861 and still in use. The post office is on the right amid a pleasant jumble of beautiful cobbled walls, warm brick and plenty of thatched roofs.

Turn left at the next road junction signposted to the beach, where there is a good view of Happisburgh Manor, an interesting 1900s house by architect Detmar Blow, over the field on the left. Its gables are embellished with the words Stella Maris and with decorative shields and escutcheons. After a short distance, turn right down a smaller lane. This is bordered by houses and bungalows on the right and an arable field on the left in the middle of which stands a red and white striped lighthouse flanked by small white cottages. The lighthouse is now kept up by a trust and is a splendid landmark on its knoll on the clifftop.

Where the metalled lane bends to the right, turn left up a track between two baulks. The track breasts the hill with an excellent view out to sea and then bends sharply to the right along a wide green way between arable fields. From here there are wonderful views to the horizon with innumerable church towers standing out above the trees and fields – a feature of this part of Norfolk.

At a junction of tracks turn left and head for the sea along an often muddy track between arable fields. Follow the well-trodden path through a field towards a line of fencing. Just before the pillbox here turn sharp left along a path along the edge of the field on the left with some scrub and then the fence and the sea beyond on the other side of the track. At the cliff edge continue walking on back to Happisburgh with the lighthouse over the field on the left. The cliff is unstable here so it is most important to keep away from the edge. Part of Eccles, the next village down the coast, has crumbled into the sea and its church is a ruin on the beach. The massive sea defences all along here testify to the dangers of erosion and flooding. Continue along the muddy path to join a small hard path the end of which has obviously dropped into the sea. The path passes a rough slipway and becomes a lane and passes a row of rather precarious looking cliffside dwellings on the right.

At a road junction opposite a postbox, turn right signposted to the beach and car park. Again there is a good view of Happisburgh Manor across the field on the left. Pass a pay and display car park on the right and carry on to the coastguard station and slipway at the end of the lane. A right of way leads through the field next to this, so bear left and go through the field next to a permanent caravan site towards the church, then leave through posts at the top, carrying on up a little lane back to the pub.

St Mary's church next to the pub is well worth a visit. Its tower is unusually tall and may have served as a beacon for ships to warn them of the dangerous Happisburgh Sands. The 15th century font and rood screen are especially notable. Its churchyard is full of the bodies of shipwrecked mariners who have come to grief on the treacherous sands and cliffs nearby. North of the church is a mound said to be the mass grave of 119 men from *HMS Invincible* which was on its way to join Nelson's fleet when it was wrecked on the sands in 1801.

27 West Runton
The Village Inn

This unusual pub looks like a cross between a bowls pavilion and an Arts and Crafts cottage. It is mainly single storied with leaded light windows, some with stained glass, a lot of dark wood inside and comfortable window seats. In front is a brick terrace and a huge lawned garden area set with tables protected from the busy road by a flint wall and flower beds, a pleasant oasis with a view of Holy Trinity church next door. The pub was the coach house for Runton House, the large building at the back of the neighbouring car park. In about 1924, it became the 19th hole of the golf course which came right up to it, but with the coming of the railway, development for holiday accommodation took over golf club land near the village. It then became the village pub in the 1940s. Since then it has had a chequered career playing host to many pop stars who came to play at the West Runton Pavilion which was part of the premises. Now it is a very pleasant and welcoming freehouse. Three open fires are a pleasant sight in winter. The pub has a traditional atmosphere enlivened with old local photographs and paintings.

113

It is popular with holidaymakers who enjoy the special atmosphere, the good food and the pleasant garden. The pub meals are delicious and there is also a separate, more up-market, restaurant menu with waitress service for those requiring more elaborate meals. A speciality on the food side is the wide variety of local fish which varies according to the time of year and availability.

There is a changing selection of real ales including Adnams Bitter. Children are welcome and dogs can be taken into the bars on leads but not into the restaurant. They are thoughtfully provided with a bowl of water outside for which my dog was most grateful.

Telephone: (West Runton) 01263 838186.

How to get there: The Village Inn at West Runton is on the main A149 coast road midway between Sheringham and Cromer.

Parking: Cars can be parked in the large car park to the side of the pub if you are using the pub facilities or at the National Trust Roman Camp car park.

Length of the walk: 4½ miles. OS Map Landranger series 144 North East Norfolk (GR 181428).

Woods and sea views characterise this walk which begins by crossing the single track railway line which is the Norwich to Sheringham and Cromer branch line. The route then skirts the golf course and Incleborough Hill to reach Roman Camp which belongs to the National Trust. From here there are spectacular views out to sea from various points in the woodland. Roman Camp is a local name for this lovely area of woods, hills and heaths. The name may have come from the site of an earthwork on one of the highest pieces of ground in Norfolk where one of a chain of beacons was sited for warning against pirates or invasion. This coastal warning system lasted intermittently from 1324 through the time of the Armada and the Napoleonic Wars up to the 19th century. Earlier the area had been used in Anglo-Saxon and medieval times for iron smelting.

The return route continues through lovely mixed woodland and along an ancient lane with more sea views back to the village. The mixed woodland is attractive to many woodland species of birds including nuthatches, willow warblers and redpoll. The scarce red squirrel is still found here, and slow worms may be seen on paths early in the morning in spring and summer.

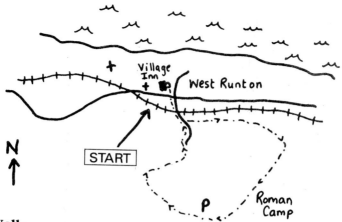

The Walk

Walk up the lane opposite the pub signposted to Aylmerton, the golf club and the Shire Horse Centre. Pass houses and shops and go over the narrow humped-back railway bridge. Continue along the road passing through an area of common land. Just before the Links Hotel, turn left down a small lane passing the golf course on the right and bungalows on the left. The lane borders the railway with the sea beyond. Follow the lane to the right as it passes through the golf course to a caravan site.

At the gates to the site, turn left along a narrow track through bushes. The track runs round the base of Incleborough Hill with the golf course on the left. When the track forks take the right hand branch continuing to skirt round the bracken covered hill. Pass Spratt's Hill and woods on the left. Just before the main path disappears into a tunnel of small trees, a white signposted public footpath goes to the right by huge old oaks. Another path just to the left of this heads straight for a radio mast rising from woods on the hill ahead. This is the route to take. It becomes a wide grassy path between two fields. The path goes through a hedgerow and passes a wooden gate into a field and then fencing on the left. The path narrows to pass through flowery banks then comes out into open fields.

Ignore the handgate leading into a camping and caravanning field on the right at a junction of paths. Continue straight ahead along a path cleared through crops towards the radio mast. The path climbs steadily up through a dark wood of conifers and huge laurel. The obvious path looks as if it becomes a rivulet in wet weather. The woods become lighter with more deciduous trees as the track meets a road at a wooden signpost.

Cross the road and take the wide stony track opposite signposted to Roman Camp. The track leads through trees passing the National Trust car park on the right opposite the Roman Camp Caravan and Camping complex where there is a tearoom. Take a small detour just beyond the car park on the right to a grassy plateau with an information board. A flag pole marks the highest point in Norfolk and benches make a pleasant stop to admire the sea views. Continue on along the track (part of the Norfolk Coast Path).

At a second parking area, take the marked (plastic arrow) path to the right of a driveway and go downhill in a cleft between wooded banks. The track becomes more grassy and there are views of the coast and meadows on the right. The small path comes out onto a broad crosstrack by a National Trust signpost.

Turn right along this (Calves Well Lane). There are more lovely views of the coast beyond the fenced and bracken-fringed meadows on the left. All Saints church at Beeston Regis has a spectacular and lonely clifftop site. The woods continue on the right and I was astonished to see a parakeet fly out of them the day I walked! The lane becomes more civilised and houses encroach. Follow it round to the left (arrow signpost) where it comes out at a little green by a road.

Turn left down the road (there is a pavement on the right to start with) passing flint cottages and then on the left is the Norfolk Shire Horse Centre and Countryside Collection, a museum of different kinds of horses and ponies which are shown at work and can be ridden or driven. Walk carefully down the road or skirt round houses through common land on the left to avoid the road, then cross over the railway bridge again to return to the Village Inn on the main road.

28 Baconsthorpe
The Hare and Hounds

The cream and green painted pub sign shows two hounds chasing a hare while the window surrounds of the building, which dates back to the 17th century, are painted to match. The pub was probably originally a farmhouse belonging to a large local estate. Homebrewed beer would have been served from the taproom, then the building would have gradually developed into a pub proper on being sold away from the estate.

The atmosphere in this unusual and welcoming hostelry is relaxed and pleasant. You enter through a cheerful porch area filled with pot plants. There is a lovely wooden serving bar made from old pine panels, and a large inglenook with a woodburning stove. Round the corner from the main bar area is a comfortable snug for families, with walls full of local pictures. Bottles and glass found in old dumps line shelves in the bar and 'Vanity Fair' prints decorate the walls.

The pub opening hours are from 11 am-3 pm and from 6.30 pm-11 pm and all day Saturday. Food is served every lunchtime and evening up to about 9.30 pm. There is an extensive specials board with the accent on fish and game which may include rabbit casserole

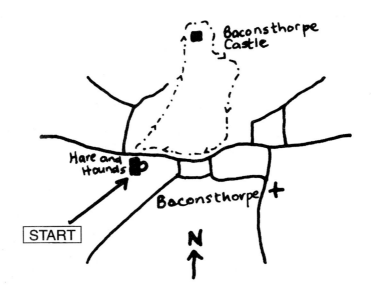

and beef in ale. Snacks such as sandwiches and ploughman's are available as well. On the autumn day of my visit a warming homemade game soup was on offer. Local game or fish may feature on the menu. Vegetarians are catered for by a delicious-sounding Mediterranean vegetable and cheese bake.

Beers include Woodforde's Wherry and Adnam's Bitter, and there may be guest beers from time to time. Strongbow cider is on draught. Dogs are welcome in the garden which is very pleasant to sit out in on warm days. Tables and benches are scattered around an informal area of grass, trees and flower and shrub beds surrounding the gravelled parking area.

Telephone: (Holt) 01263 712340.

How to get there: The Hare and Hounds is on the outskirts of the straggling village of Baconsthorpe which is just over 2 miles out of Holt signposted from the A148.

Parking: There is parking at the pub or at Baconsthorpe Castle, which is signposted at the other end of the village from the pub.

Length of the walk: About 3½ miles. OS Map Landranger series 133 North East Norfolk (GR 115372).

Baconsthorpe village is reached by a maze of tiny lanes and feels almost lost in the rural Norfolk countryside, which has helped to keep its old-fashioned and unspoiled atmosphere. The walk follows green lanes beginning just opposite the pub to reach the splendid ruins of Baconsthorpe Castle (owned by English Heritage), set in the midst of farming activity out towards the parish of Bodham. The site of the castle is particularly beautiful as it is moated on three sides with a small lake on the fourth. There are lovely views over fields and farmland edged with hedges and fringed with trees. The return route goes along footpaths through farmland which have been diverted slightly but are fairly well marked. It then passes through the village which straggles along a long main street from the church at one end to the pub at the other. There are longer walks in the area starting from Holt Country Park or Mannington Hall both of which are well worth a visit.

The Walk

Walk down stony Hall Lane just opposite the pub passing a few cottages on the left and then a piggery and a deep pond on the right. Another stony track veers to the left, but this walk carries straight on along a hedged track marked by plastic arrows on a post on the right. Follow the lane bearing a little to the right. Ignore another track which branches off to the right, keeping ahead until Baconsthorpe Castle comes into view. Go through a gateway and continue along a stony track with open fields on the right and a hedge on the left. Hall Farm here is on the site of an ancient hall house now demolished.

Turn right by the farm and then left into the castle precincts, walking through a series of metal kissing gates to explore the ruins, the main part of which is surrounded by a beautiful moat. Baconsthorpe Castle was a large moated and semi-fortified house built by the Heydon family in the 15th century, though its name suggests that it may have been started earlier by the Bacon family from nearby Gresham. The remains include inner and outer gatehouses and a curtain wall. An information board explains that during the comparative security of Tudor times the Heydon family made Baconsthorpe the centre of a vast sheep run. The east range was transformed to contain a woollen industry within the castle walls. Weavers would have worked in the upper storey by enlarged windows. By 1600 the family fortunes had declined and after the Civil War most of the castle was demolished and sold as building material, though in 1781 the outer gatehouse was still being used as a dwelling and the courtyard was a walled garden. John Heydon who began the building in the 15th century was a cunning lawyer prospering at the expense of others in the harsh climate of the Wars of the Roses. The great inner gatehouse was probably completed before his death in 1480. His heir Sir Henry Heydon finished the work by 1486. The impressive remains are built of flint with stone quoins and there is later brick and tile work with decorative stone facings.

Leaving the castle, turn left down the wide concrete farm road, then take a signposted right turn over an unusual A-shaped bridge with a little decorative lead capped roof. Cross a stile and follow the path through fields with a ditch on the left hand side. Pass a sewage works, go through a gap in fencing, cross a small footbridge and then a stile. Bear rightish round the edge of a field. At the corner of the field cross another small bridge and a stile with an arrow marker and turn right. Go round the edge of the next field bearing left at the corner and again at the next corner, then almost immediately right by a signpost. Go over a stile by a metal gate and on to the main street of Baconsthorpe village opposite an old Wesleyan chapel.

To visit the church, which forms an attractive group on the easterly outskirts of the village with the old rectory of 1770, take a detour down the street to the left then bear right. The church contains a monument dated 1592 to Sir William Heydon, some interesting brasses, a fine Easter Sepulchre and a 13th century piscina.

Otherwise, for the main walk continue on along the main street to the right past a turn to Edgefield on the left. The road leaves the village proper and passes through fields skirting an old pond or moat on the left and then Pitt Farm, finally reaching the Hare and Hounds again.

29 **Wiveton**
The Bell

The charm of the Bell lies in its rural position standing with just a few cottages on a small crossroads overlooking Wiveton green and the church of St Mary the Virgin. This cottagey, whitewashed freehouse is 600 years old, almost as old as its neighbour the church, and it must have been a busy place when the nearby river Glaven was a large tidal estuary with a quay and a boat builder's yard. Now it is a pleasant spot for holidaymakers and locals to relax in. There are tables outside in the back garden with views of the church and children are allowed here and in the spacious modern conservatory. Inside, the pub is furnished in traditional fashion.

The food is good with simple dishes such as rack of lamb and Danish specialities including gravadlax. Sandwiches are included on the à la carte menu, and further offerings are written up on a specials board. The excellent children's menu features real, not junk, food. The beers are Adnam's and various guest beers, with Strongbow cider on draught.

Telephone: (Cley) 01263 740101.

How to get there: The Bell is on the green at Wiveton, which is a mile off the A149 coast road between Blakeney and Cley.

Parking: The pub has no car park but there is plenty of room to park on the green.

Length of the walk: 4 miles mainly along small lanes. OS Map Landranger series 133 North East Norfolk (GR 041429).

The valley of the little river Glaven is an especially beautiful area. It has an air of tranquillity and timelessness. As you walk from the green towards late 13th century Wiveton Bridge and look out over the lush marsh fringed meadows of the valley it is difficult to picture the bustling scene in medieval times when boats could come up to the nearby quay to load and unload and when magnificent ships were built for the service of Queen Elizabeth I in the boat builder's yard. The walk turns up a small lane leading to the village of Glandford with its picturesque ford, mill and shell museum. A footbridge takes pedestrians over the water for a short detour to explore this attractive village and tiny St Martin's church rebuilt in late Victorian times. The walk then turns away from the river and passes through undulating rural countryside and woods, with spectacular views out over the marshes to the sea.

The Walk

Turn left out of the pub at the crossroads, and walk towards the church following the lane signposted to Weybourne and Sheringham. Notice the cannon barrel complete with cannon ball on a mound just here. Pass the church of St Mary the Virgin on the left, with its fine flint work outside and perpendicular interior, and pause to look inside at the pictures of 15th and 16th century ships carved into the stone walls reviving echoes of when Wiveton was busy with sailors and merchants, industry and trade. Then go down into the valley crossing the river Glaven via the ancient stone bridge. There once was a chapel of the Holy Trinity incorporated into the south west corner of the bridge. From here there are lovely views of Cley church on the left and the sails of Cley windmill appear over a huddle of cottages. It is likely that there was a harbour below the bridge right back in Roman times, part of the Blakeney Haven. There would have been a huge sheet of tidal water stretching between the churches of Wiveton and Cley, edged with busy wharves.

Turn right along a lane signposted to 'Glandford and Unbridged Ford'. On the right a stand of poplar trees delineates the marshy meadow by the river – a good area for frogs, dragonflies and butterflies. On either side of the narrow lane there are hanging branches of dog roses and blackberries springing from a dense hedgerow – a haven for wildlife.

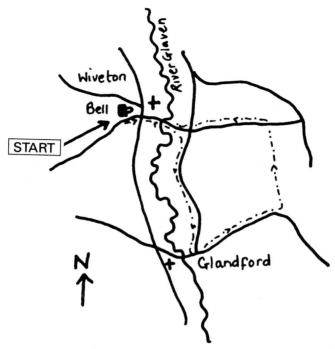

Where the road bends to the left, take a short detour to the right to the ford and footbridge to look at the enchanting picture of Glandford Mill downstream with the broad mill pond swarming with quantities of ducks and geese. Cross the footbridge to visit Glandford village, church and shell museum if desired.

Return to the corner. On the right a wooden gate leads into the Bayford Estate which is managed for conservation purposes and which has waymarked paths. For this walk bear left at the corner and continue on uphill along a lane with well kept hedges on either side. Soon there are views out to sea over Cley windmill and the churches. Pass a sand and gravel works on the right.

Where the lane bends sharply to the right and a green lane goes ahead, turn left into a field and walk along its edge with a bank of scrub and trees on the right. Again there are wide views of Wiveton, the marshes and the sea. Go through a gap in the hedge and continue on along the edge of the next open field towards woodland along an overgrown and uneven path. Go ahead into the wood up a gentle slope following an obvious path, rather overgrown with branches at head height. Keep climbing on uphill through the middle of a rather sparse copse (Lavender Hill). Leave the wood and continue straight on through heathland along a fairly obvious path. The bracken, rosebay willowherb and gorse edging Hammer Hill Nature Reserve were nearly at head height in July. The path then wends its way downhill through more scrub to reach a gap in a fence. Go ahead into a field and walk down the left hand boundary hedge. The path leads over two wooden bars near a footpath sign onto a road.

Turn left along the road past a bungalow called Thornhill. Wiveton church stands up well ahead. Go over the crossroads and retrace your steps over the bridge and uphill back to the pub.

Binham
The Chequers

Standing at a crossroads near the green in Binham, the 300 year old Chequers inn presents an attractive picture with its mellow flint walls and pantiled roof. Pubs of this age usually have an interesting history and there is talk of an underground passage leading from the pub to the priory (perhaps for monks who couldn't be seen to visit the tavern in the normal way!). It is said that the ghost of a previous landlord's young child can be seen behind the bar and in the upstairs rooms. Unusually, the building and its acre of land belong to the village and are leased to the landlord, the revenues providing a charity for the community.

The Chequers is now the only pub left in the village and provides an excellent service including morning coffee and en suite non-smoking accommodation. Food is available lunchtime and evening each day. The extensive menu has an emphasis on locally produced food, seafood and game, though vegetarians are not forgotten. Opening times are 11.30 am to 2.30 pm and 5.30 pm to 11 pm (Monday to Saturday) and 12 noon to 3 pm and 7 pm to 10.30 pm (Sunday), while food is served from 12 noon to 2 pm and 6 pm to 9 pm (7 pm to 9 pm Sunday).

The pub is a freehouse and has a good selection of real ales including Adnams Bitter, Woodforde's Norfolk Wherry and a guest ale. A wide range of keg beers, lager and cider is available. The

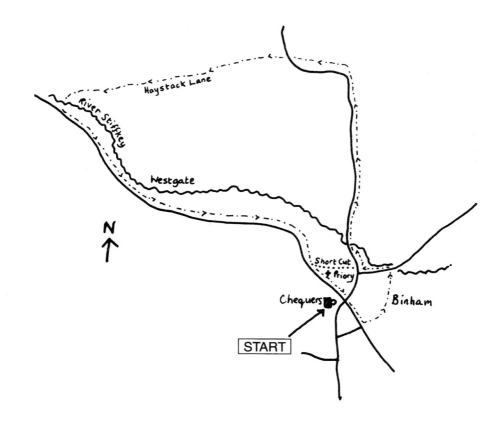

cosy one-roomed bar is open plan but blazing fires provide a respite from cold winter winds. A no-smoking rule applies in the restaurant area and there are several smoke extractors throughout the pub. Children are welcome and there is a pleasant walled garden area to sit out in as well as tables at the front of the pub. The furnishings are mainly modern but settles give an old-fashioned feel and the inglenook is embellished with horse brasses.

Telephone: (Binham) 01328 830297.

How to get there: Binham is about 5 miles south east of Wells-next-the-Sea in north west Norfolk down a turning off the B1105 between Wells and Little Walsingham.

Parking: At the pub or next to the nearby green.

Length of the walk: About 3½ miles of fairly easy walking. OS Map Landranger series 132 North West Norfolk (GR 982397).

The exciting Norman ruins of Binham priory dominate this walk which explores some of the surrounding footpaths and lanes with their extensive views over rolling Norfolk countryside. The priory remains are superb and plenty of time should be allowed to look round them, concentrating particularly on the nave which is preserved and used as the parish church of St Mary and the Holy Cross. The 12th century priory church is built of flint and limestone brought from Barnack by river and sea, on a site dominating the river Stiffkey which fed the nearby monks' fishponds and a watermill. The Benedictine priory was founded by a nephew of William the Conqueror, Peter de Valoines, the most powerful man in the eastern counties. It was a cell of St Albans abbey which led to much wrangling and even fighting throughout the centuries leading up to the Dissolution when it became the property of the Paston family. A short cut can be taken from the main walk through the site. The village itself has some very interesting houses (some built from stone rifled from the priory ruins) and a range of shops and services which make it almost self sufficient.

The Walk

On leaving the pub cross the road and follow the lane ahead which leads alongside the green with its village sign on the right. Continue past the general stores, also on the right, to a second green with the base of an old stone market cross on it. This was the site of an annual four-day fair granted by charter by Henry I and of weekly markets. Bear left at a road junction, then turn into the yard at Manor Barn and take the signposted (plastic arrow on post) footpath bearing right along a broad stony track. The track bears round to the left and carries on between tree-studded hedgerows with lovely views over the priory ruins in the gaps of the hedge on the left. At the bottom of the track bear left to the road and turn left along it towards the priory in the distance. Where the road bends to the left turn right along a lane signposted to Cockthorpe and Stiffkey by Riverside House.

For a very short cut through the ruins, at the junction of the road from Langham where the main walk goes to the right, cross a stile on the left which leads through undergrowth to another stile. Go over this and bear slightly right across the meadow towards the ruins making for a metal kissing gate by a tall ruined pillar to the right of the nave. Go through this and pick your way ahead through the ruins to another kissing gate. Bear right, go down a path and through another gate and then through the broken arch onto the road. Turn left back to the pub.

For the main walk, continue on over white railinged Carroll's Bridge with more lovely views of the priory on the left. Pass red brick Ford House with its flood marker post outside and continue uphill. Follow the road round to the left (lovely views again) and where the road bends sharply to the right, bear left along a wide track (Haystack Lane) between hedges and continue on for some distance. Follow the track downhill towards a pantiled house. Keep the house on the left and go ahead over a stile into a meadow walking ahead by a hedge on the right and the little river Stiffkey on the left. The footpath here seems to have been diverted further away from the house. After a short while look out for a wooden footbridge. Turn left across this and continue ahead across the meadow dipping down into a ditch and up again towards a small gap in the hedge where a wooden footpath signpost can just be seen.

Cross the stile here opposite Short Lane Farm and turn left down the road which has a nice wide verge on the left. Pass a turning to Wighton on the right on the outskirts of Binham. Walk along the pavement on the left into the village, passing a lovely selection of cobbled, knapped flint and pantiled cottages (many of the old houses in Binham have been built using material from the priory ruins). Continue on past extensive farm buildings to the priory main entrance under a broken arch. The whole priory site is of high architectural value deserving a close look, and the remaining part of the great church is full of interesting features. Of especial note is the richly decorated west end with its great window. The abbey is in the care of English Heritage. Continue on along the road passing the decorative flint and red brick Abbey House back to the pub.